THE COMPLETE BOOK OF
NUMBERS &
COUNTING

AMERICAN
EDUCATION
PUBLISHING™

Columbus, Ohio

Copyright © 2004 School Specialty Publishing. Published by American Education Publishing™, an imprint of School Specialty Publishing, a member of the School Specialty Family.

Printed in the United States of America. All rights reserved. Except as permitted under the United States Copyright Act, no part of this publication may be reproduced or distributed in any form or by any means, or stored in a database or retrieval system, without prior written permission from the publisher, unless otherwise indicated.

Send all inquiries to:
School Specialty Publishing
8720 Orion Place
Columbus, OH 43240-2111

ISBN 1-57768-604-7

8 9 10 11 WAL 10 09 08 07

Table of Contents

Number Recognition

Place Value

Counting

Number Recognition

Name ____________________

Number 0

Color the number. **Color** the word.

0

zero

Name _____

✏️ **Trace** the number. **Trace** the word.

0

zero

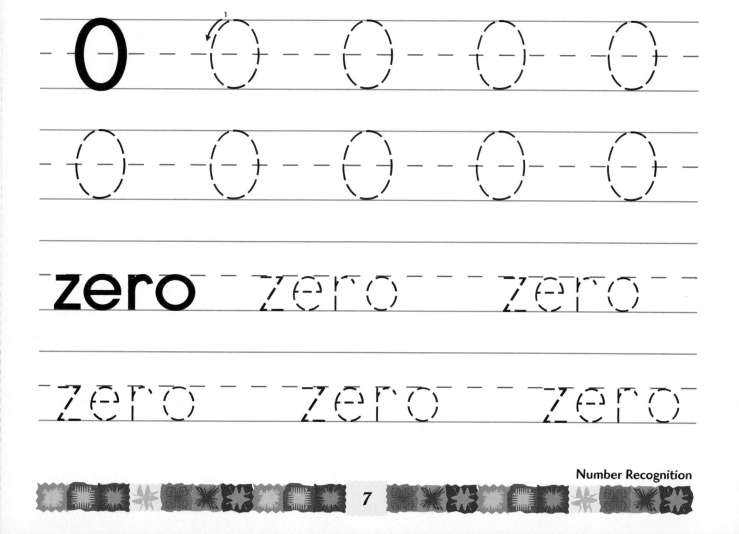

Name _____

Now practice **writing** the number and the word by yourself on the lines below.

0

zero

Name _____

Number

 **Color** the number. **Color** the word. **Color** the rest of the picture.

Number Recognition

✏️ **Trace** the number. **Trace** the word.

1

one

one one one

one one one

Now practice **writing** the number and the word by yourself on the lines below.

1

one

Name _____

Have fun with 1!

✏️ **Trace** the big 1. ✏️ **Circle** and **draw** 1. **Color** the pictures.

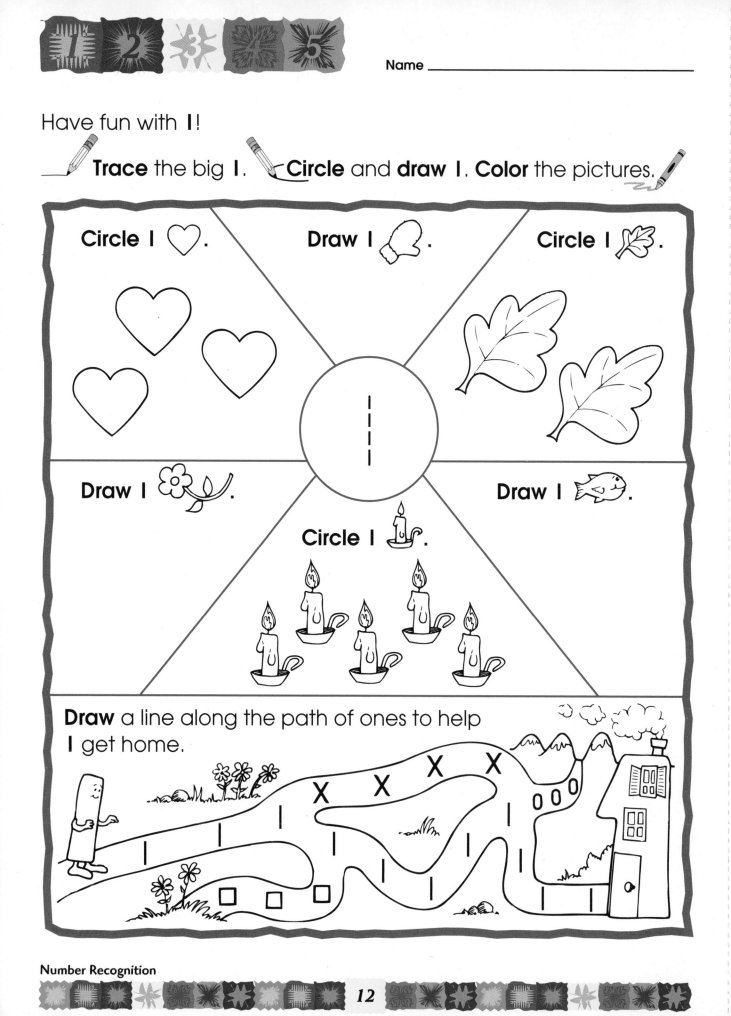

Circle 1 ♡.

Draw 1 🧤.

Circle 1 🍂.

Draw 1 🌸.

Draw 1 🐟.

Circle 1 🕯️.

Draw a line along the path of ones to help 1 get home.

Name _____

Count and color.

Trace each 1. Color 1 red, 1 blue,

1 green. Circle each group of 1.

Name _____

One of a Kind

Color the spaces: 1 - green • - brown one - blue

What is it?

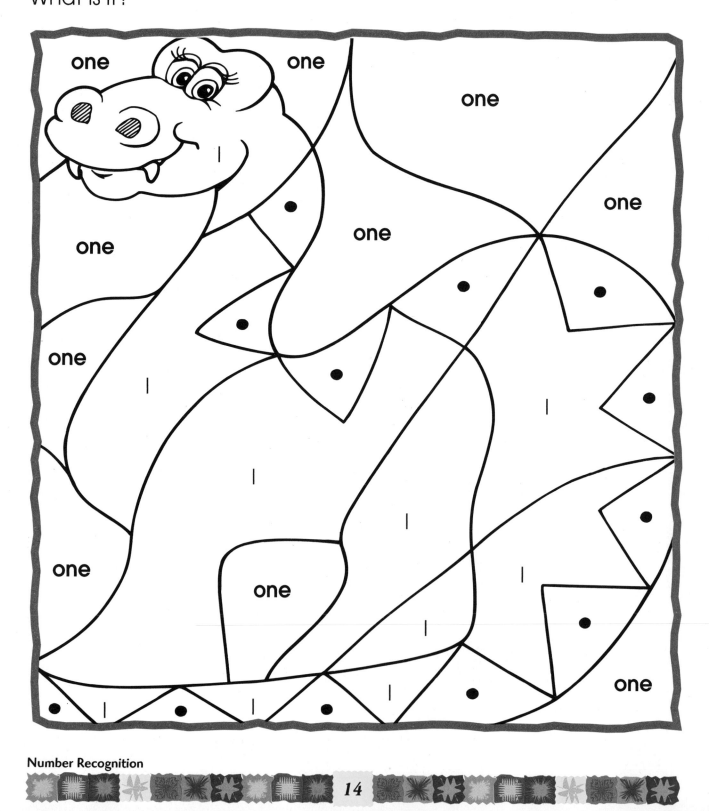

Number

Name _____

Color the number. **Color** the word. **Color** the rest of the picture.

✏️ **Trace** the number. **Trace** the word.

2  two

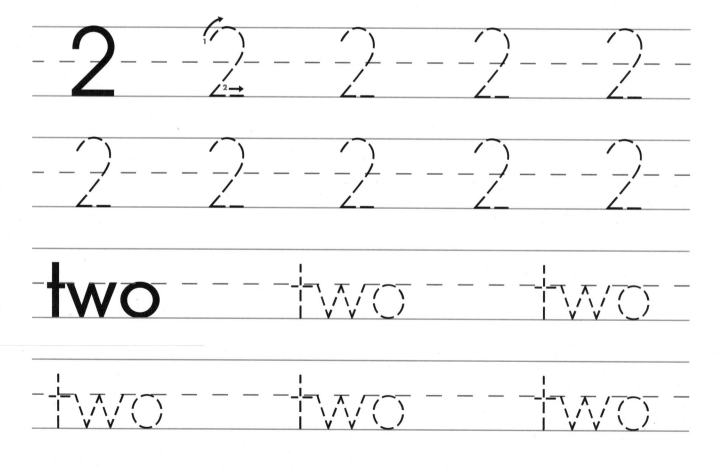

Name _____

Now practice **writing** the number and the word by yourself on the lines below.

2

two

Number Recognition

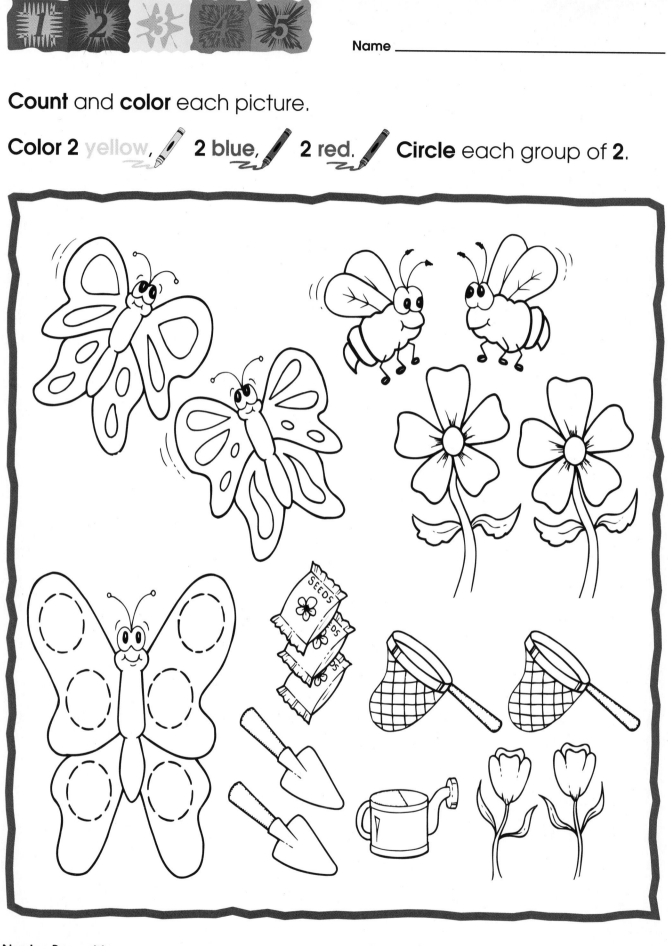

Name _____

Count and color each picture.

Color 2 yellow,   2 blue,   2 red.   Circle each group of 2.

Name _____

More to do with 2.

Trace each **2**. **Color** the flowers: **2 red**,  **2 purple**, **2 yellow**. **Circle** each 🐛 with a **2**.

Name _____

Very cool!

Color the spaces: **2 - black**   two - blue   I - white
• • - orange

What is it?

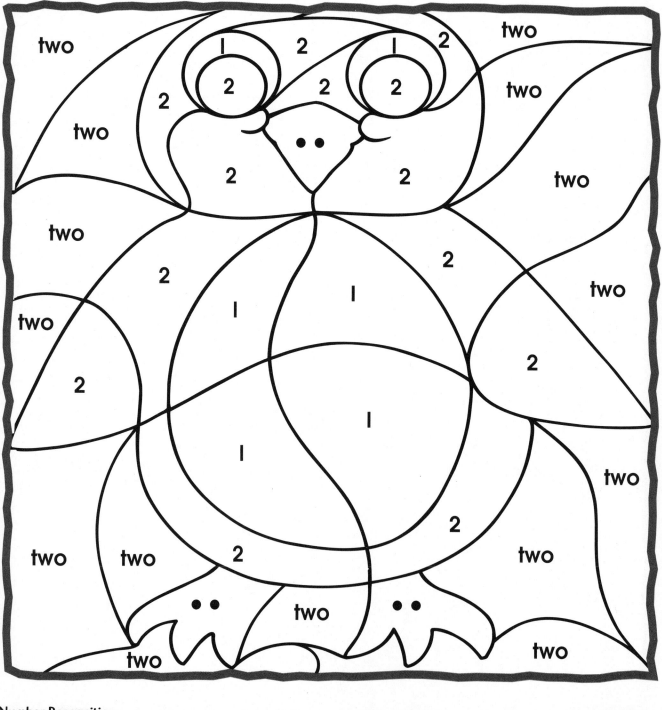

20

Number

Color the number. **Color** the word. **Color** the rest of the picture.

Trace the number. **Trace** the word.

3

three

3   3   3   3   3

3   3   3   3   3

three three three

three three three

Number Recognition

Name _____

✏️ Now practice **writing** the number and the word by yourself on the lines below.

3

three

Circle each group of **3**. **Color** the whole picture.

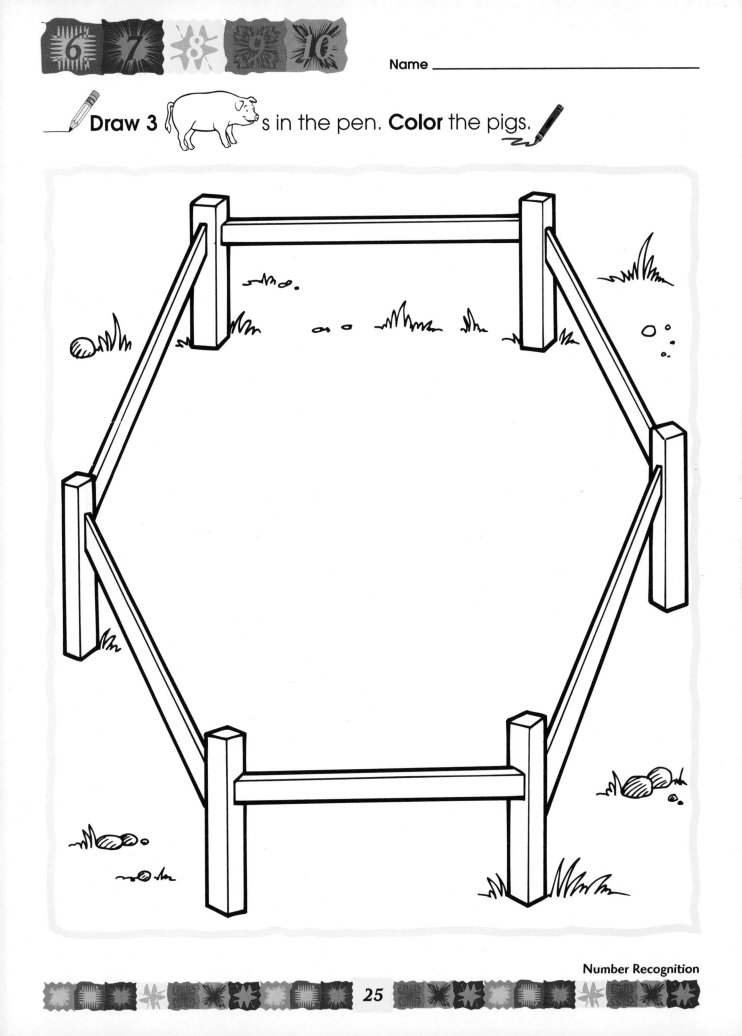

Name _____

Draw 3 🐖s in the pen. **Color** the pigs.

Name _____

✏️ **Circle 3** things in each group. **Color** the pictures that are circled.

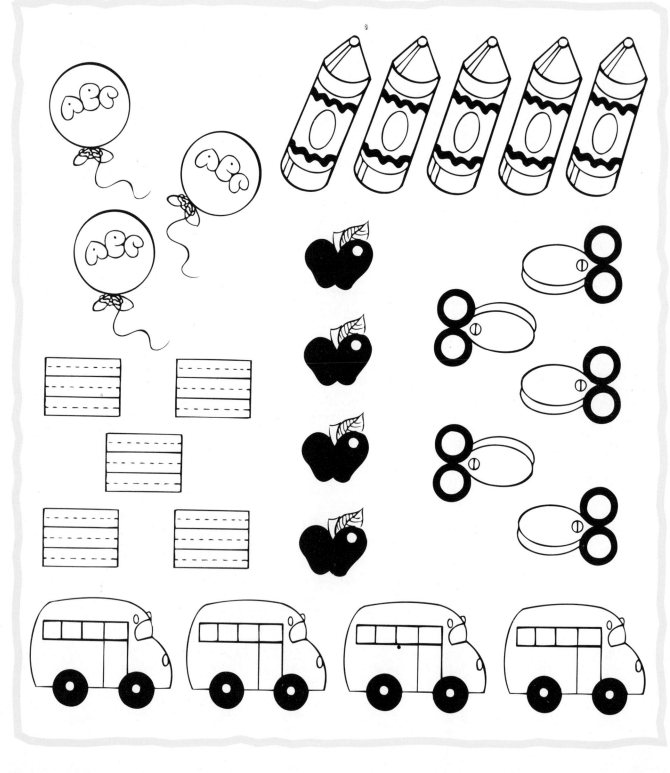

Name _____

Number

4

Color the number. **Color** the word. **Color** the rest of the picture.

Name _____

✏️ **Trace** the number. **Trace** the word.

4   four

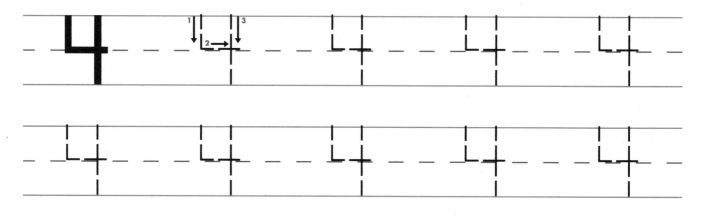

four   four   four

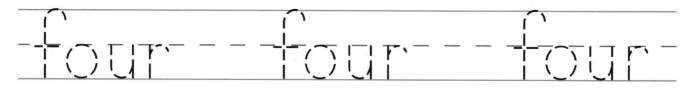

four   four   four

Number Recognition

Name _____

Now practice **writing** the number and the word by yourself on the lines below.

4

four

Name _____

Circle 4 things in each group. **Trace** each 4. **Color** the picture.

Name _____

Where are the **4**'s hiding?

Circle the **4**'s. **Color** the picture.

Name _____

Very cool!

Color the spaces: **4** - yellow   :: - orange   **four** - blue
3 - black

What is it?

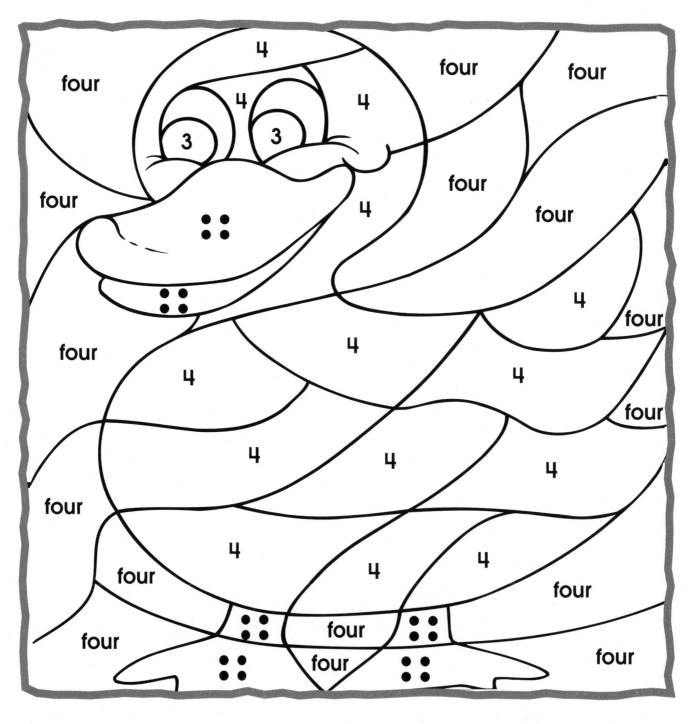

Number Recognition

32

Number

Color the number. **Color** the word. **Color** the rest of the picture.

Name _____

Name _____

✏️ **Trace** the number. **Trace** the word.

5   five

5   5   5   5   5

5   5   5   5   5

five   five   five

five   five   five

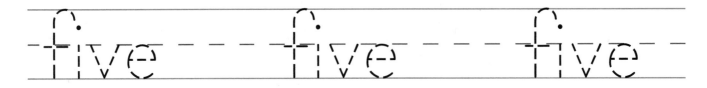

Name _____

Now practice **writing** the number and the word by yourself on the lines below.

5

five

Number Recognition

Name _____

Color **5** scoops of ice cream **pink**, **5** scoops **brown**, and leave **5** scoops **white**.

Name _____

Draw an **X** on each group of **5** dolphins diving through a hoop!

Name _____

Count and **color** each picture. **Trace** the dotted line from **1**-**5**. **Circle** each group of **5**.

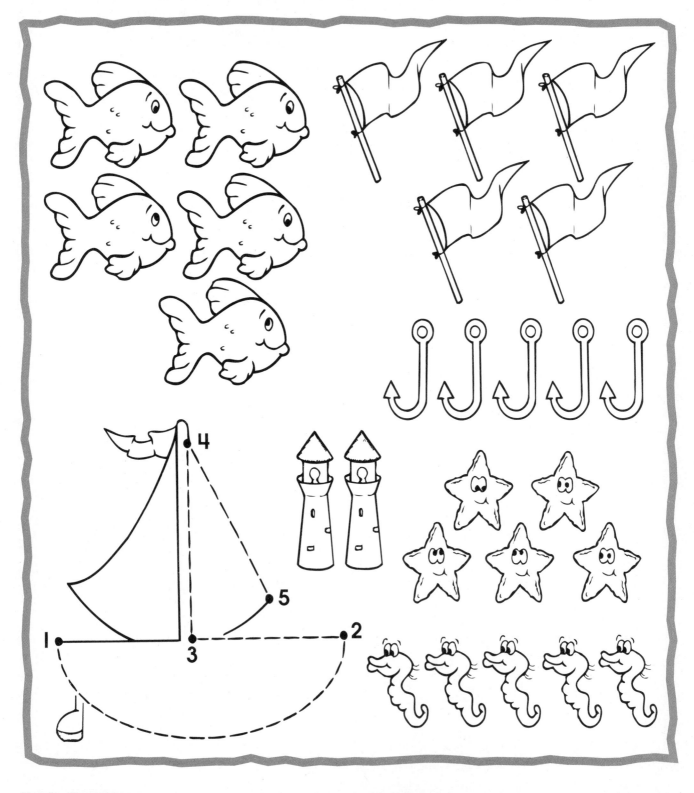

6

Name _____

Trace the numbers and words. Practice **writing** the numbers on the line below.

0 1 2 3 4 5

0 1 2 3 4 5

- - - - - - - - - - - - - - - - -

zero zero one

one two two

three three four

four five five

39

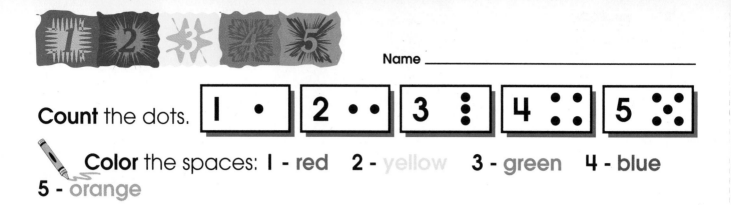

Name _____

Count the dots.　|1 •|　|2 • •|　|3 ⋮|　|4 ⋮⋮|　|5 ⋮∴|

Color the spaces: 1 - red　2 - yellow　3 - green　4 - blue
5 - orange

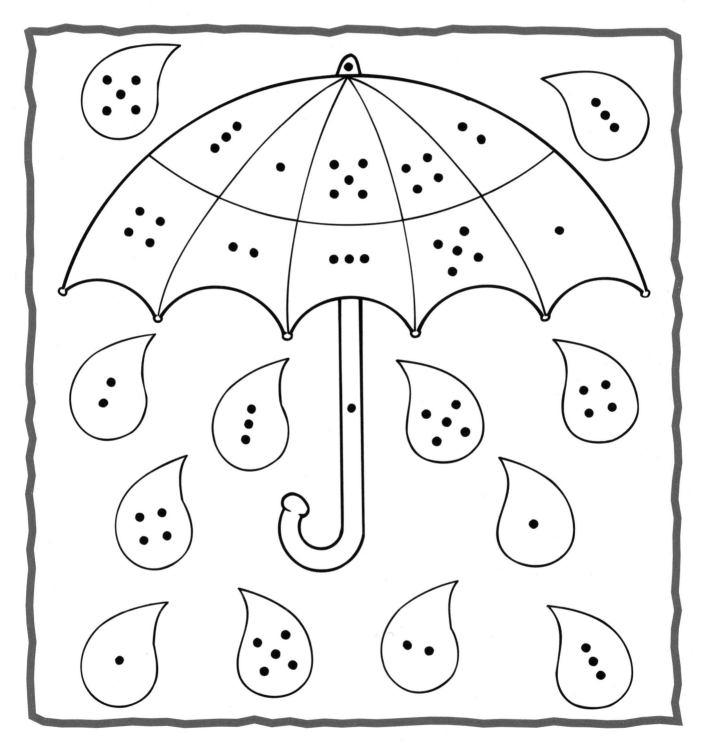

How many?

✏️ **Trace** the correct number for each box. **Color** all the pictures. 🖍️

Name _____

Count each set of pictures.

Write the number in the boxes below. **Color** the pictures.

How many?

Name _____

Color the spaces: **1 - red**   **2 - blue**   **3 - yellow**   **4 - green**
5 - orange

Name _____

Trace the dotted line from **1-5** on each picture. **Color** the picture.

Name _____

Count each group of vegetables. **Write** the number in the box.
Color the vegetables, too.

0 1 2 3 4 5

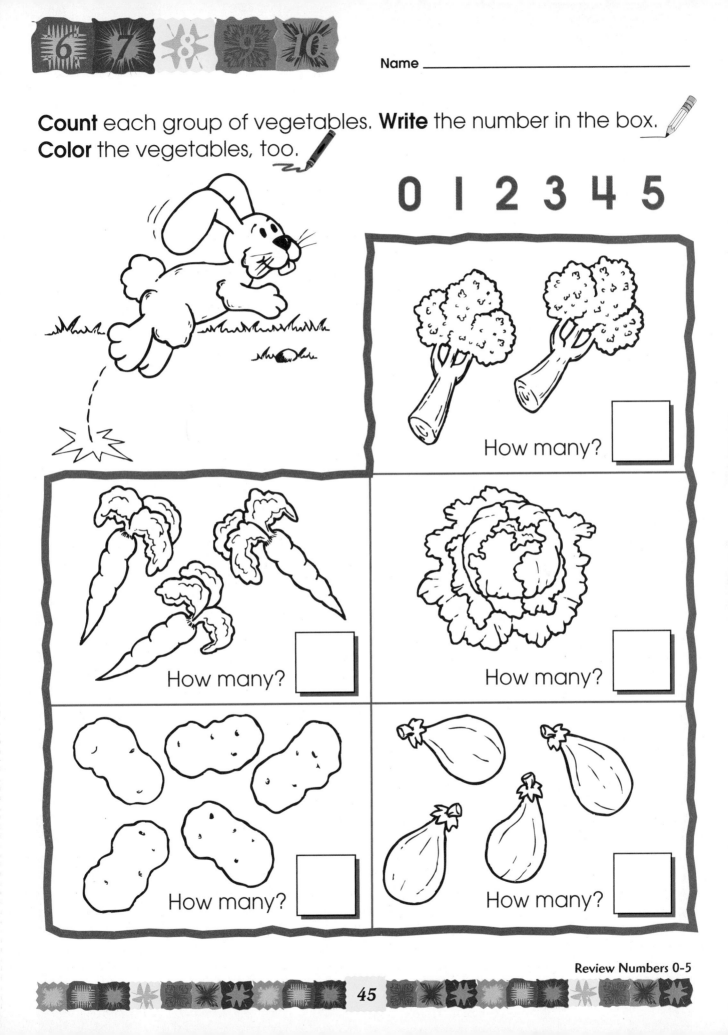

How many? ☐

How many? ☐

How many? ☐

How many? ☐

How many? ☐

Name _____

Color the spaces: **1 - blue**   **2 - yellow**   **3 - green**   **4 - red**
5 - purple

What is it?

Name _____

Trace the dotted line from **1-5**.
Color the picture.

See where
5 🐟 live.

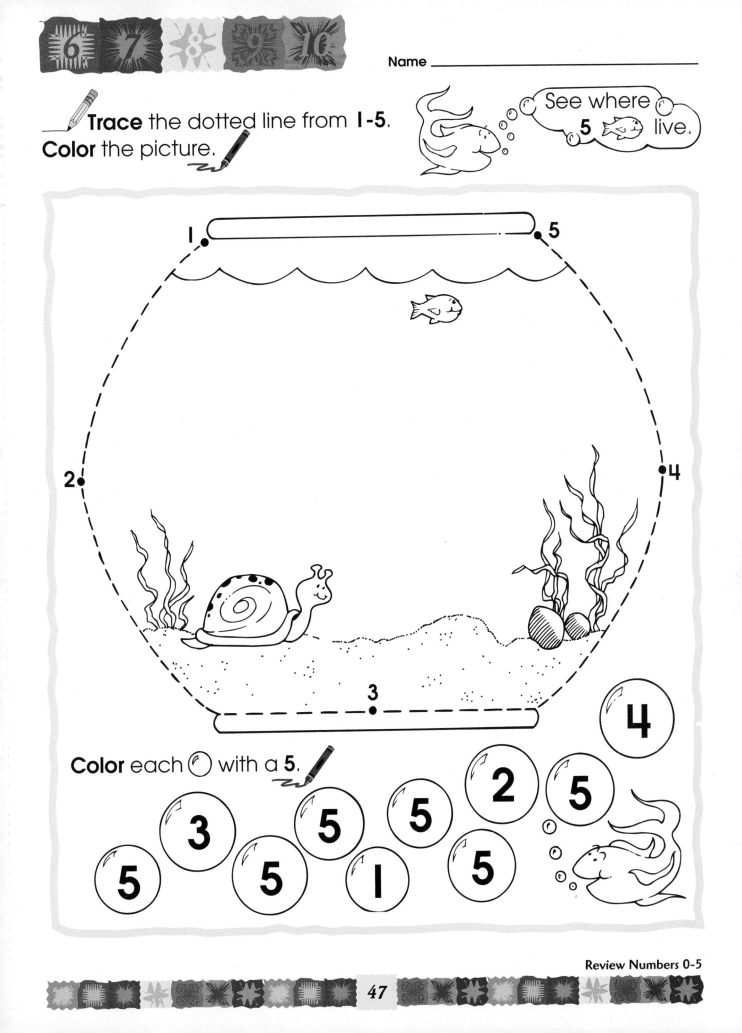

Color each ⃝ with a **5**.

Name _____

Color the spaces: 5 - white 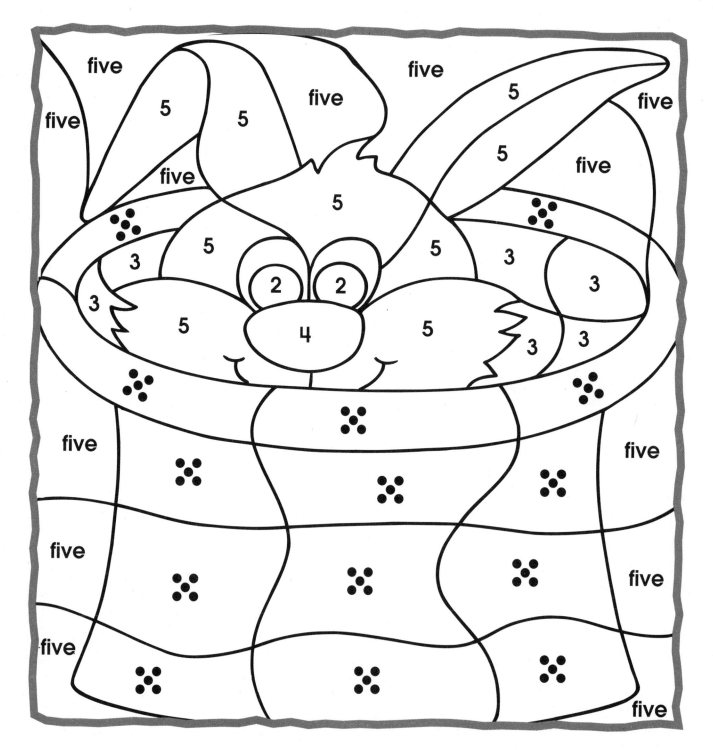 - black five - red 4 - pink
3 - yellow 2 - blue

What is it?

Trace the dotted line from **one** to **five**. **Color** the picture.

What is it?

two •

three •

one

four

five •

Name _____

Count the pictures. ✏️ **Trace** the numbers and words. **Draw** a line to match.

1 one

2 two

3 three

4 four

5 five

Name _____

Circle the number words in the puzzle. The first one is done for you. Color the picture.

zero
one
two
three
four
five

f	e	o	f	i	v	e
t	h	r	e	e	b	t
x	o	n	e	s	i	w
f	o	u	r	a	d	e
z	e	r	o	t	w	o

Review Numbers 0-5

Name _____

How many?

Circle the correct number in each group. **Color** the pictures.

1   2   3

2   3   4

0   1   2

3   4   5

Name _____

2   3   4

3   4   5

1   2   3

3   4   5

3   4   5

1   2   3

Name _____

Look at the picture below.

How many do you see? **Write** the number in the box. **Color** the pictures.

Number

Color the number. **Color** the word. **Color** the rest of the picture.

Name _____

Trace the number. Trace the word.

6  six

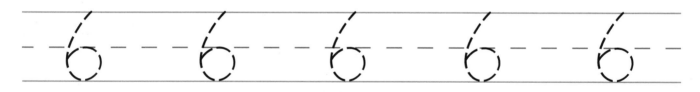

six

six

Now practice **writing** the number and the word by yourself on the lines below.

6

six

Name _____

Count and **color** each group of pictures. **Trace** the dotted line from **1-6**. **Circle** each group of **6**.

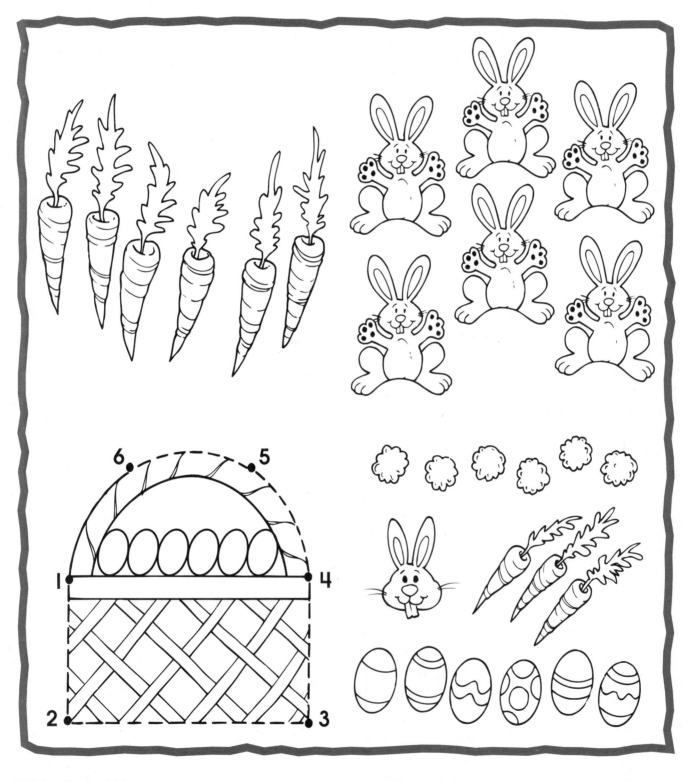

Name _____

Pop a snack!

Color the spaces: **6 - white** :::- green **six** - yellow **5 - red**

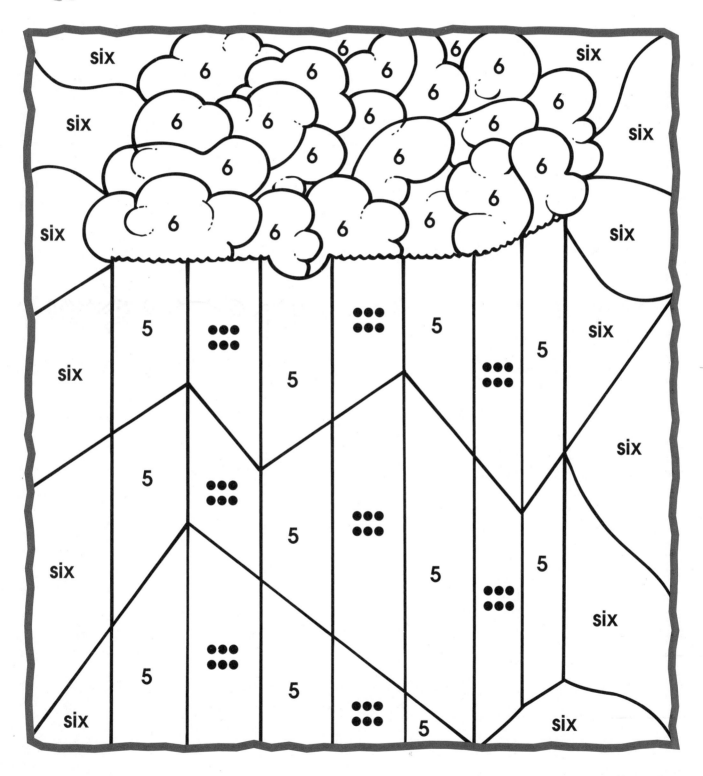

Name _____

Where are all the **6**'s?

Circle the **6**'s. **Color** the picture.

How many 🐰 ? ☐

Number

Name _____

7

Color the number. **Color** the word. **Color** the rest of the picture.

✏️ **Trace** the number. **Trace** the word.

7

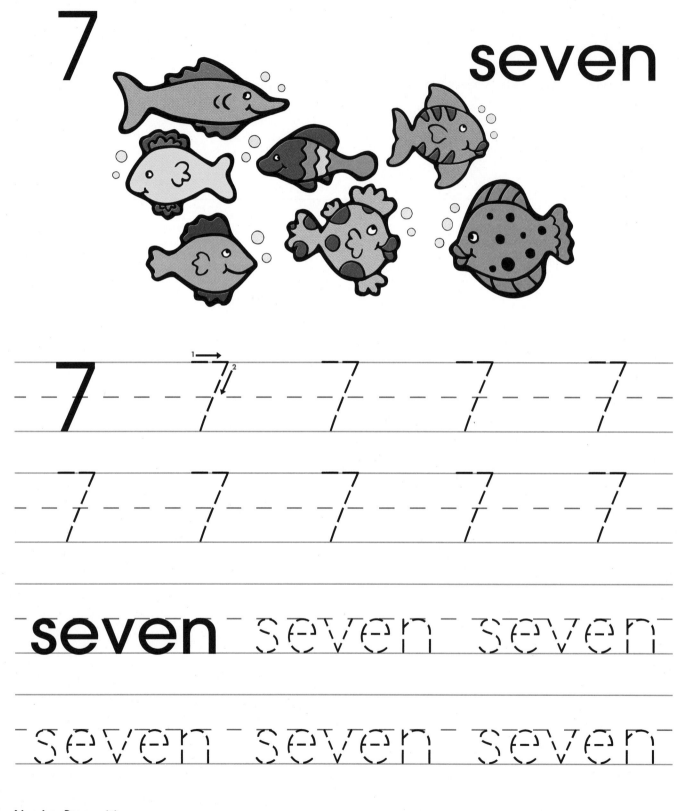

seven

7

7 7 7 7 7

7 7 7 7 7

seven seven seven

seven seven seven

Name _____

Now practice **writing** the number and the word by yourself on the lines below.

7

seven

Where are all the **7**'s?

Circle the **7**'s. **Color** the picture.

How many  ?

Name _____

Count and **color** each group of pictures. **Trace** the dotted line from **1-7**. **Circle** each group of **7**.

Trace the dotted line from **1-7**.
Draw 7 apples on the tree.

It's heaven, when I find **7**.

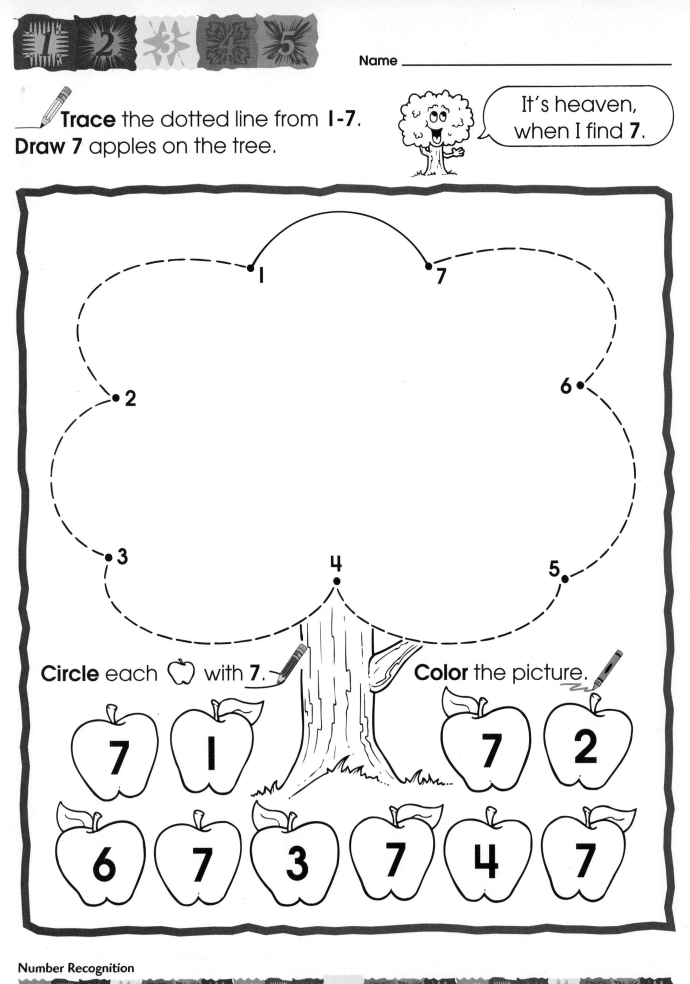

Circle each 🍎 with **7**.

Color the picture.

Name _____

Number

Color the number. **Color** the word. **Color** the rest of the picture.

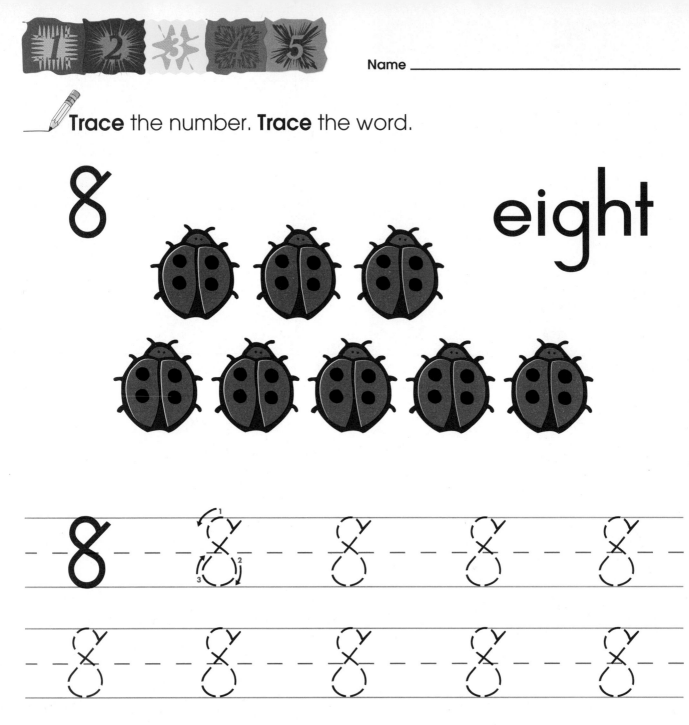

✏️ **Trace** the number. **Trace** the word.

8   eight

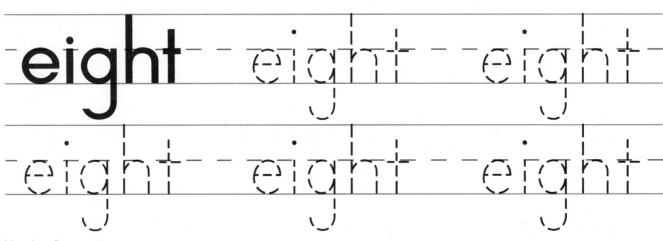

Name _____

Now practice **writing** the number and the word by yourself on the lines below.

8

eight

Name _____

Color the spaces: **8** - *yellow*   ●●●● - **red**   **eight** - *green*

What is it?

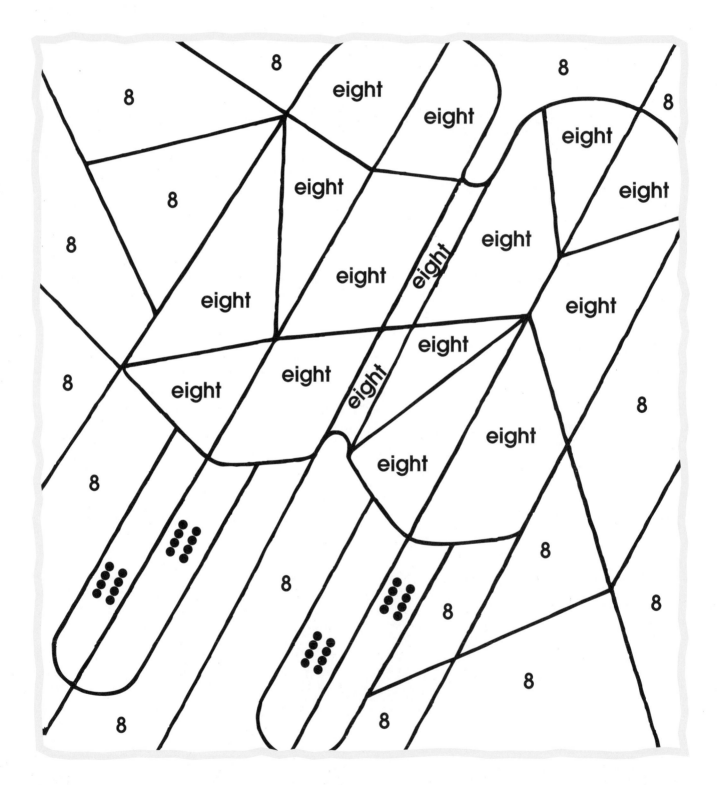

Name _____

Draw 8 s on the . Color the picture.

Number Recognition

Name _____

Number

Color the number. **Color** the word. **Color** the rest of the picture.

9

nine

Name _____

✏️ **Trace** the number. **Trace** the word.

q   nine

q   a   a   a   a

a   a   a   a   a

nine   nine   nine

nine   nine   nine

Name _____

Now practice **writing** the number and the word by yourself on the lines below.

9

nine

Name _____

Count and **color** each picture. **Trace** the dotted lines from **1-9**. **Circle** each group of **9**.

Name _____

Color the spaces: **9** - white **::::** - blue **nine** - red

What is it?

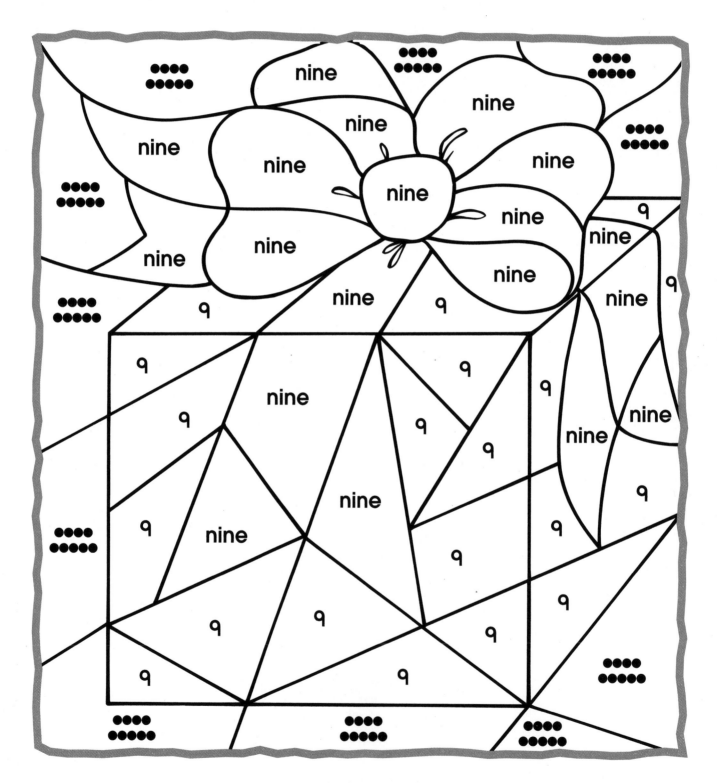

Number Recognition

76

Name _____

Number

Color the number. **Color** the word. **Color** the rest of the picture.

✏️ **Trace** the number. **Trace** the word.

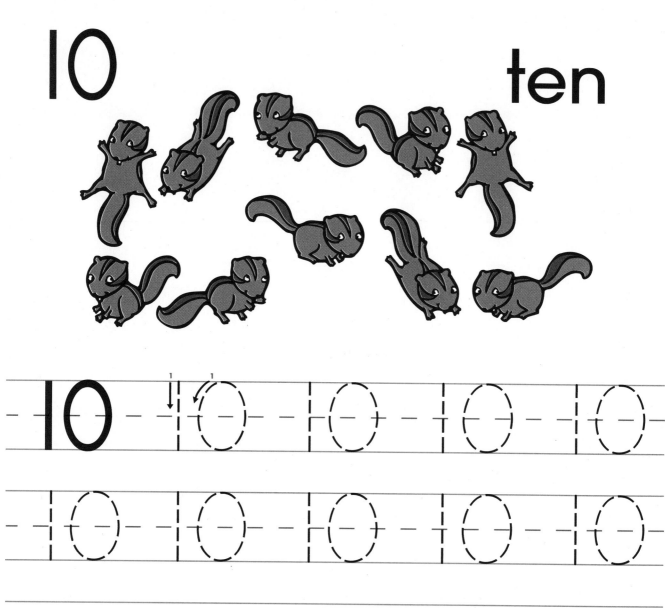

10   ten

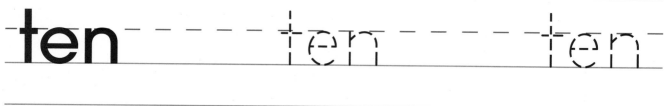

10 10 10 10 10

10 10 10 10 10

ten ten ten

ten ten ten

Number Recognition

Name _____

Now practice **writing** the number and the word by yourself on the lines below.

10

ten

Name _____

Draw 10 😊s on this shirt. **Color** the picture.

Name _____

Where are the **10**'s?

✏ **Circle** the **10**'s. **Color** the picture. ✎

How many s? ☐

Name _____

✏️ **Trace** and **write** the numbers and the words. Practice writing the numbers on the line below.

0   1   2   3   4   5

6   7   8   9   10

zero zero one one

two two three

three four four

Name _____

✏️ **Trace** and **write** the numbers and the words. Practice writing the numbers on the line below.

five   six

seven   eight

nine   ten

0 1 2 3 4 5

6 7 8 9 10

Name _____

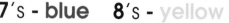 **Color** the spaces: **6**'s - **red**   **7**'s - **blue**   **8**'s - yellow
9's - **green**   **10**'s - orange

Name _____

Read each number word. **Write** the matching number on the cone.

0 1 2 3 4 5 6 7 8 9 10

seven   nine   two   five

three   ten   six

zero   one   eight   four

Name _____

Color the correct number of things in each row.

Name _____

Too many objects!

✏️ **Draw** an **X** on the extra objects in each group.

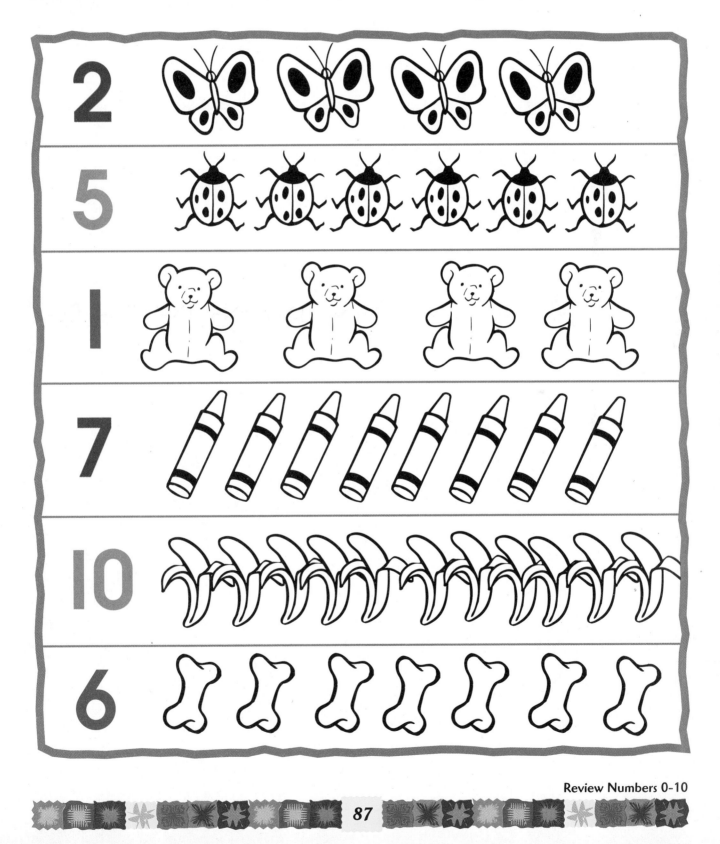

Name _____

Count. Use the code to **color** the pictures to match the number on each towel.

1 - green   2 - yellow   3 - blue
4 - red   5 - orange   6 - brown
7 - purple   8 - gray   9 - black

Name _____

Color the correct number of marbles in each bag.

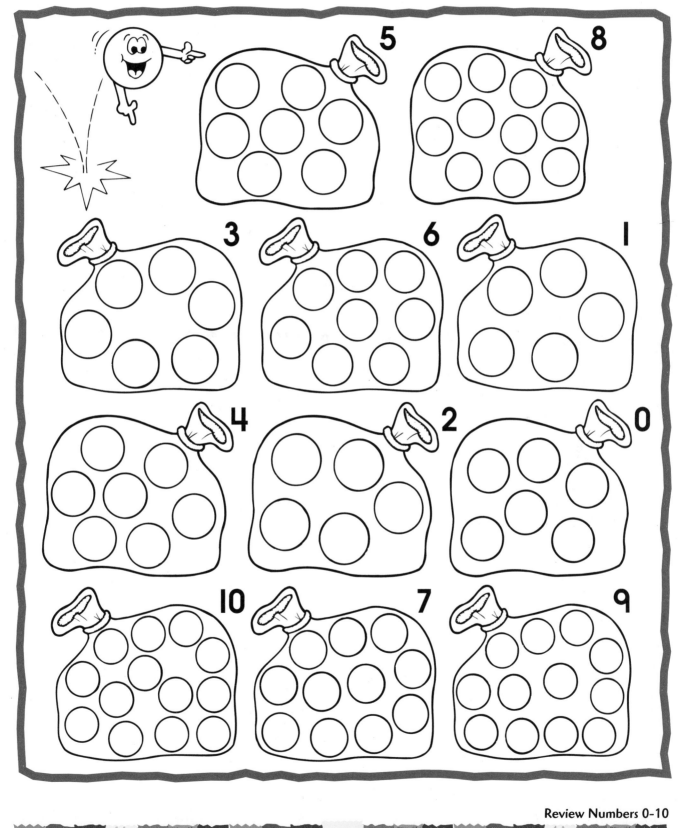

Find the hidden numbers **0-10**.

Circle the numbers. **Color** the picture.

Name _____

 **Draw** a line from each  to the correct number word.

 1

 6

 2

 7

three
six
one
seven
two
five
ten
eight
nine
four

 3

 8

 4

 9

 5

 10

Review Numbers 0-10

Name _____

Count each group of animals. ✏️ **Draw** a line from the number to the correct number word. The first one is done for you.

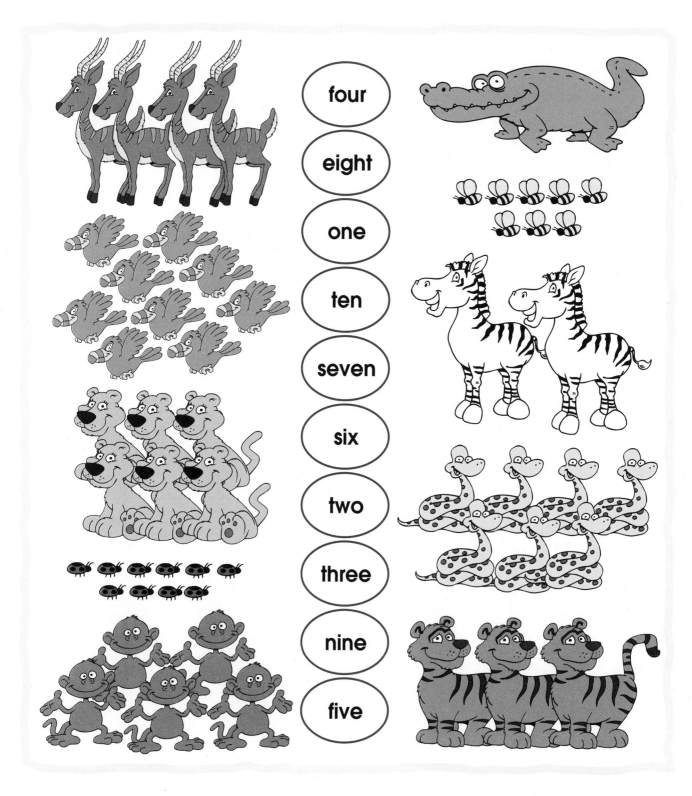

four

eight

one

ten

seven

six

two

three

nine

five

Name _____

Connect the dots from **1-10. Color** the picture.

What is it?

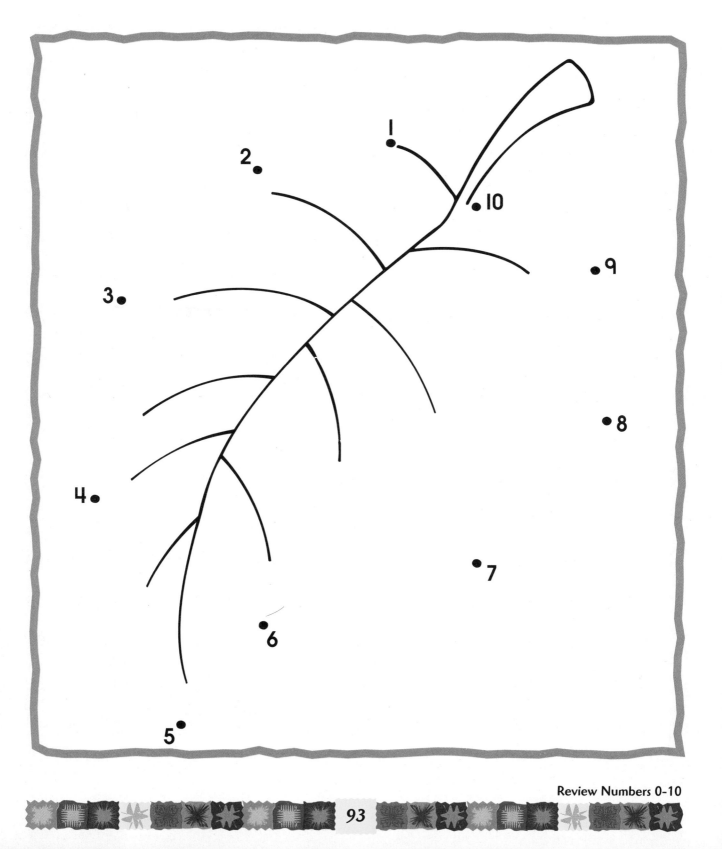

Name _____

Count the pictures in each group. **Circle** the number. **Color** the pictures.

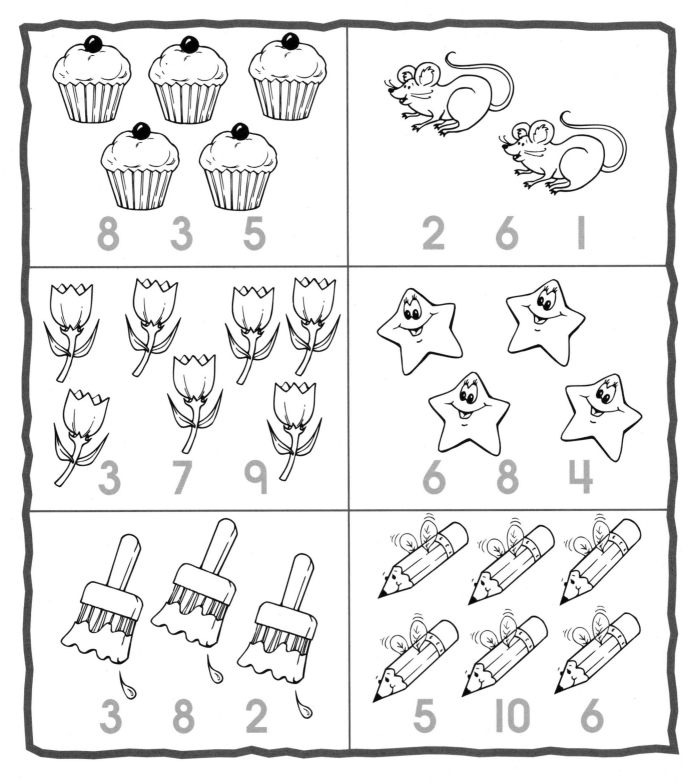

Name _____

Trace the dotted line from **1-10**. **Draw** and **color** a picture on Teddy's shirt.

1 2 3 4 5 6 7 8 9 10

Decorate my shirt!

Name _____

Color the number. **Color** the correct number of objects in each row.

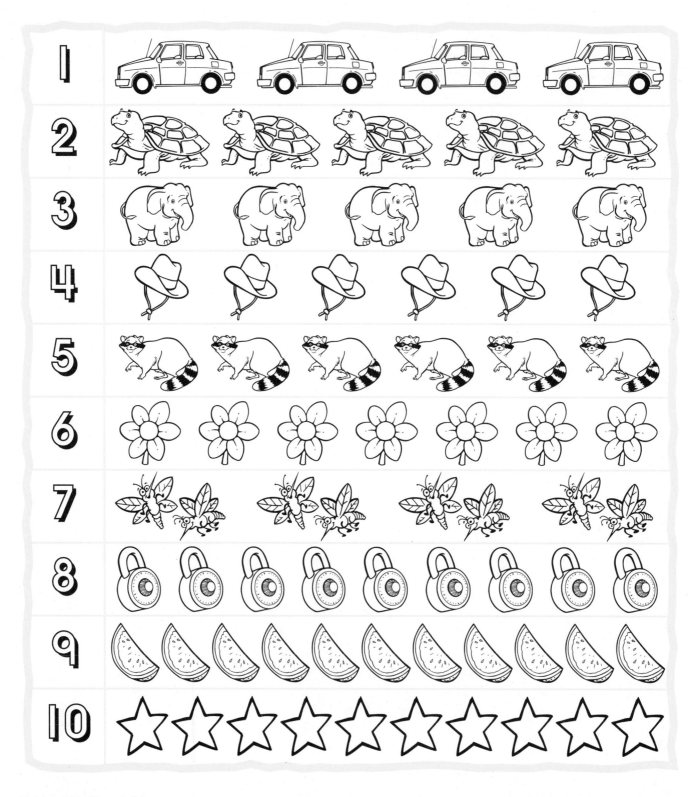

Name _____

Count the dots. |6| ::: |7| ::: |8| ::: |9| ::::: |10| :::::

Color 6 - purple   7 - green   8 - orange   9 - blue   10 - yellow

Name _____

✏ **Write** the missing numbers on each pencil.

1 2 3 4 5 6 7 8 9 10

Good work!

Name _____

Count the pictures in each group. **Circle** the number.
Color the pictures.

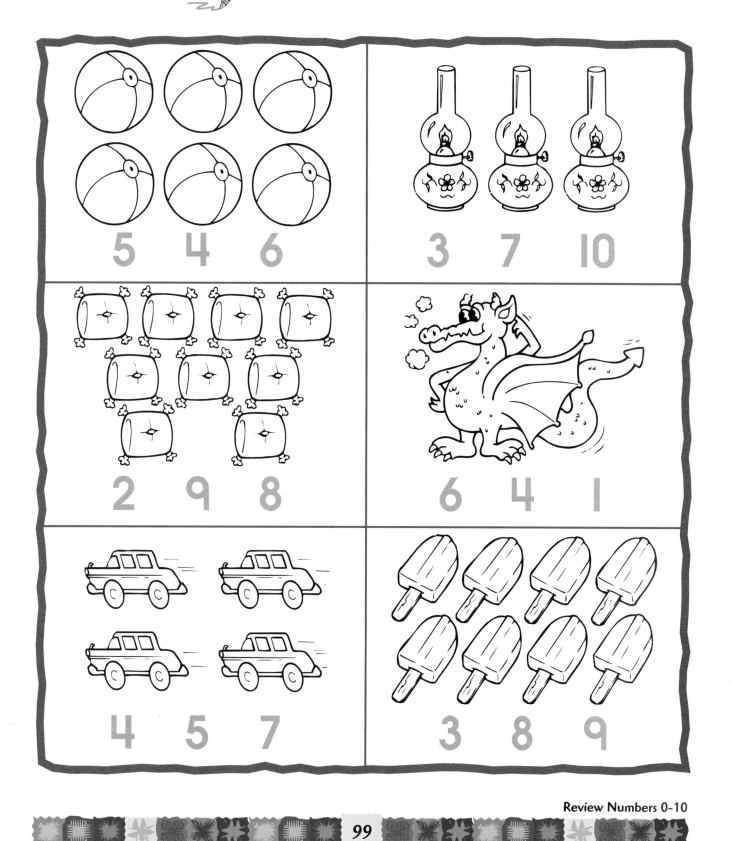

5 4 6

3 7 10

2 9 8

6 4 1

4 5 7

3 8 9

Name _____

Color each number. Draw an **X** on each letter.

100

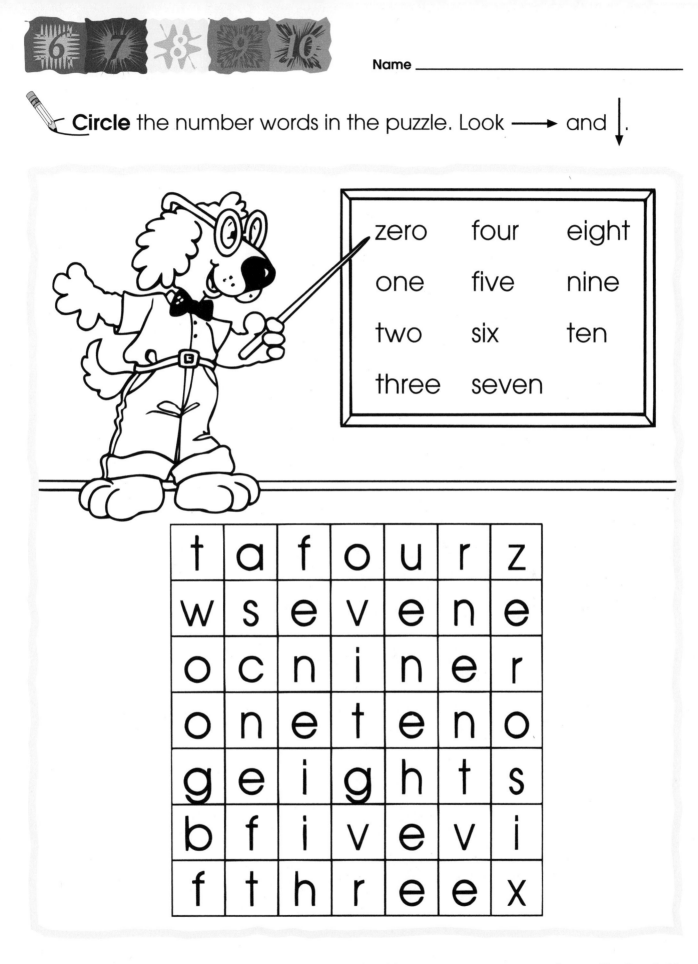

Name _____

Circle the number words in the puzzle. Look ⟶ and ↓.

zero	four	eight
one	five	nine
two	six	ten
three	seven	

t	a	f	o	u	r	z
w	s	e	v	e	n	e
o	c	n	i	n	e	r
o	n	e	t	e	n	o
g	e	i	g	h	t	s
b	f	i	v	e	v	i
f	t	h	r	e	e	x

Name _____

Count the number of each thing in the picture. ✏️ <u>**Write**</u> the number on the line.

Name _____

Count the sheep on the hill. 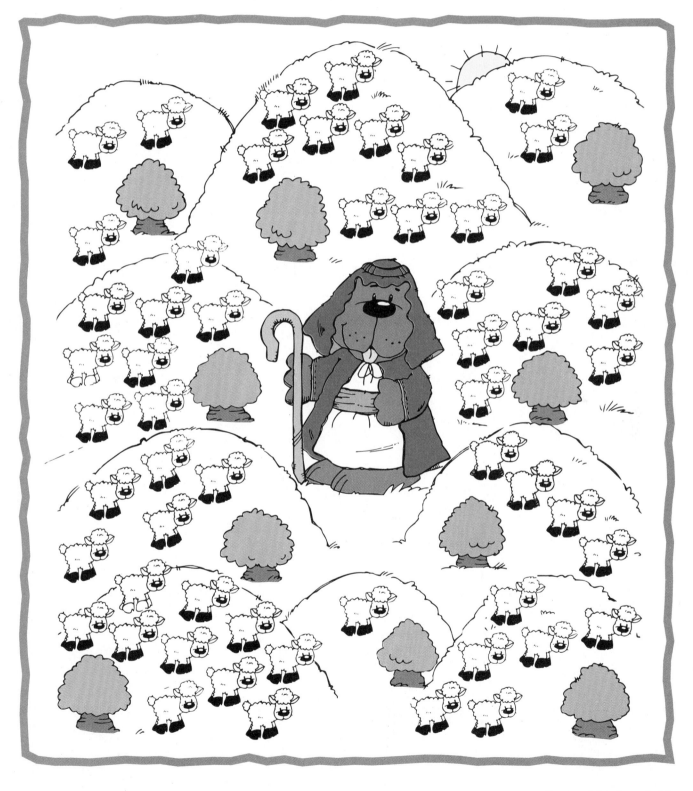 Then, **write** that number on each tree.

Review Numbers 0–10

103

Name _____

Number

Color the number. **Color** the word. **Color** the rest of the picture.

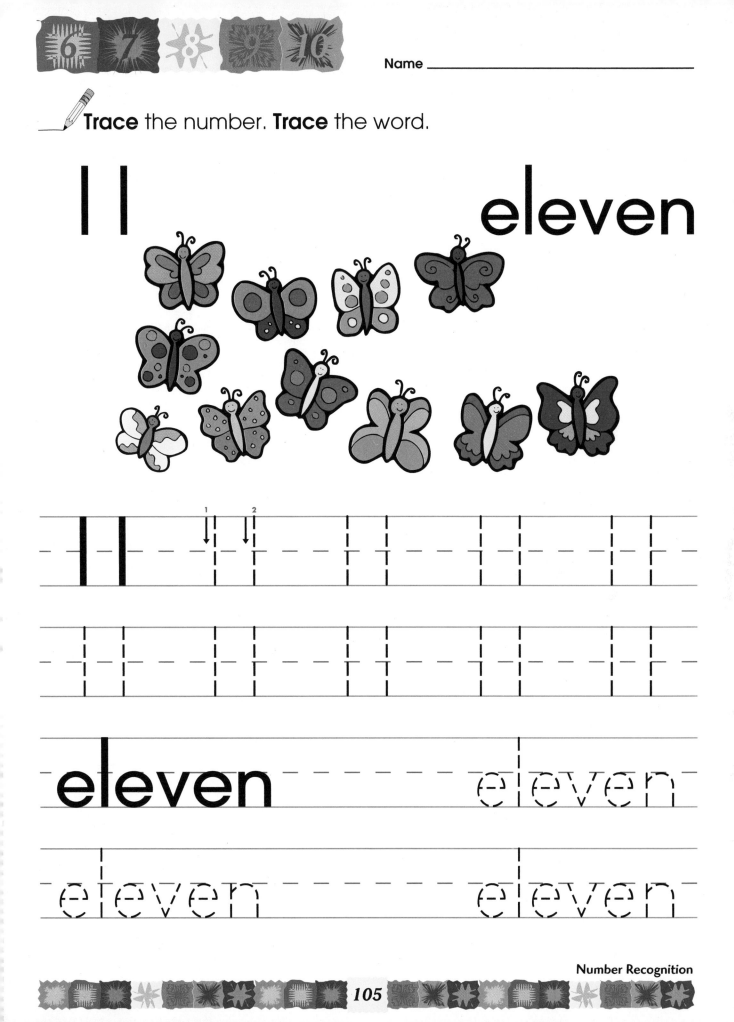

Name _____

✏️ **Trace** the number. **Trace** the word.

11

eleven

11

eleven   eleven

eleven   eleven

Name _____

Now practice **writing** the number and the word by yourself on the lines below.

11

eleven

Number Recognition

Name _____

Elmo the Elephant juggles all day long.

____ **Draw** and **color 11** balls for Elmo to juggle today. Don't forget to **color** Elmo, too!

Name _____

Number

12

Color the number. **Color** the word. **Color** the rest of the picture.

12

twelve

Name _____

✏️ **Trace** the number. **Trace** the word.

12   twelve

12   12   12   12   12

12   12   12   12   12

twelve   twelve

twelve   twelve

Name _____

Now practice **writing** the number and the word by yourself on the lines below.

12

twelve

Number Recognition

Name _____

Ted Turtle plays a terrific tune on his tuba.

Color 12 notes for Ted to play. Color Ted.

Name _____

✏️ **Write** the missing numbers on each snake.

1 2 3 4 5 6 7 8 9 10 11 12

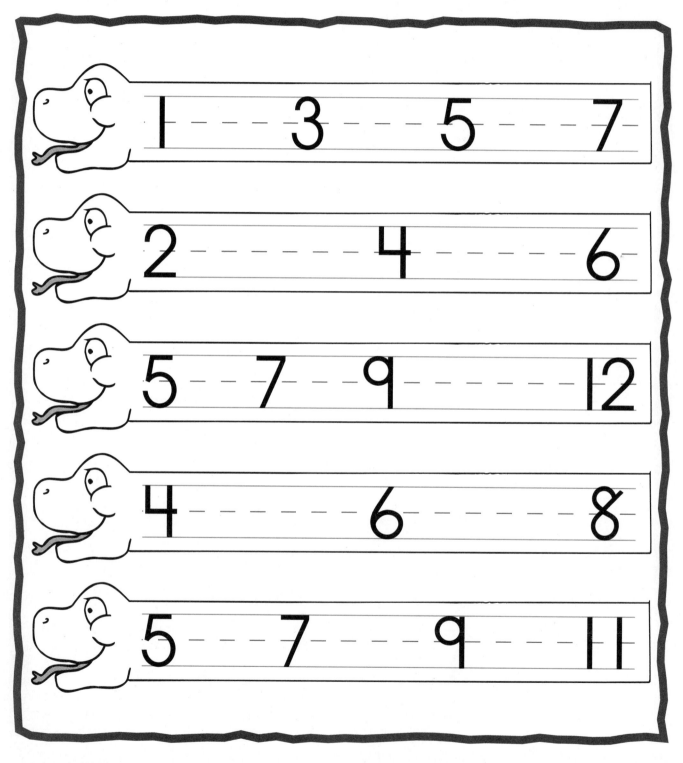

Number

Color the number. **Color** the word. **Color** the rest of the picture.

✏️ **Trace** the number. **Trace** the word.

13   thirteen

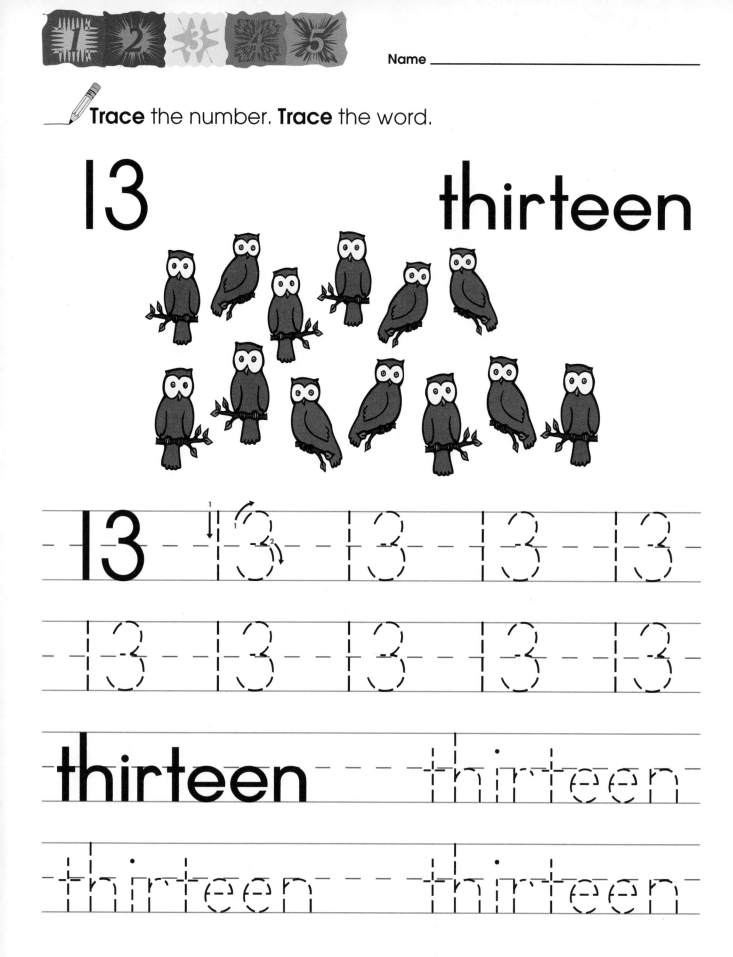

13   13   13   13   13

13   13   13   13   13

thirteen   thirteen

thirteen   thirteen

Name _____

✏️ Now practice **writing** the number and the word by yourself on the lines below.

13

thirteen

Draw 13 donuts in the bakery box. **Color** the donuts to match your favorite flavors.

Number

Color the number. **Color** the word. **Color** the rest of the picture.

✏️ **Trace** the number. **Trace** the word.

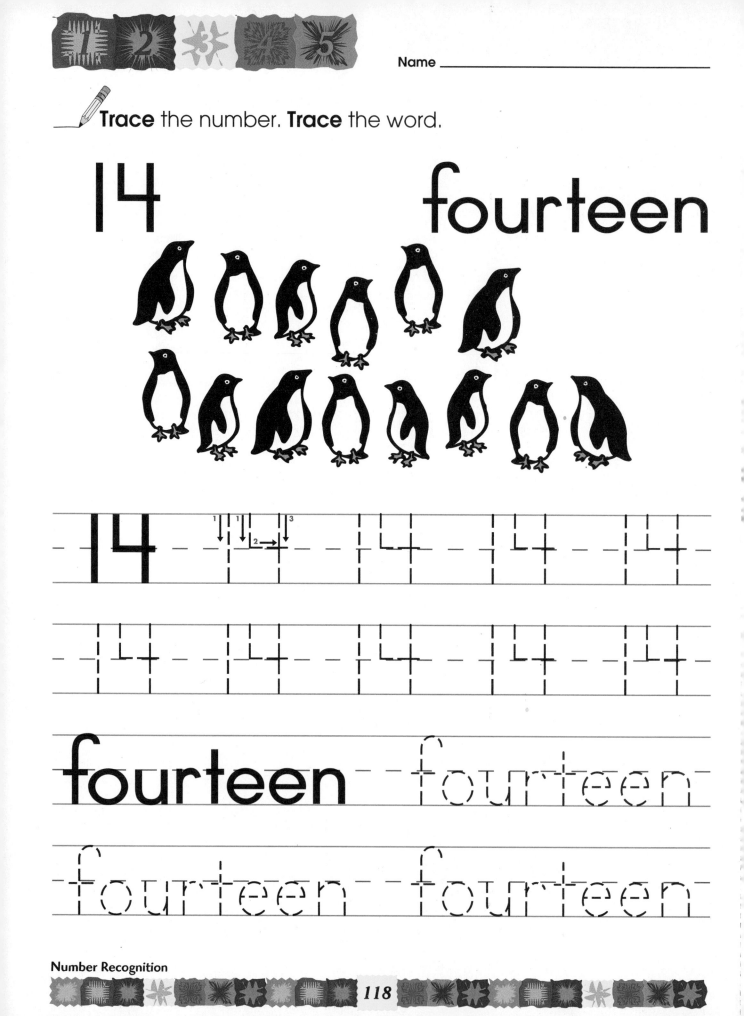

14   fourteen

Now practice **writing** the number and the word by yourself on the lines below.

14

fourteen

Name _____

How many?

✏️ **Circle** the correct number for each box.

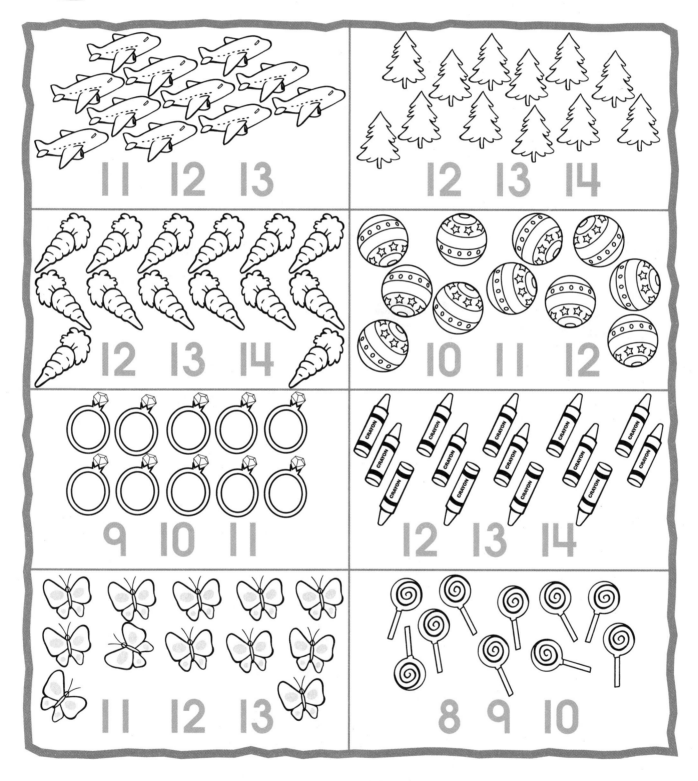

Number Recognition

120

Number

Color the number. **Color** the word. **Color** the rest of the picture.

Name _____

Number Recognition

Name _____

Trace the number. Trace the word.

15   fifteen

15   15   15   15   15

15   15   15   15   15

fifteen   fifteen

fifteen   fifteen

Number Recognition

Now practice **writing** the number and the word by yourself on the lines below.

15

fifteen

Name _____

Draw **15** bows on the tail of the kite! **Color** the kite and bows with bright colors!

Name _____

✏️ **Connect** the feet in number order.

1 2 3 4 5 6 7 8 9 10 11 12 13 14 15

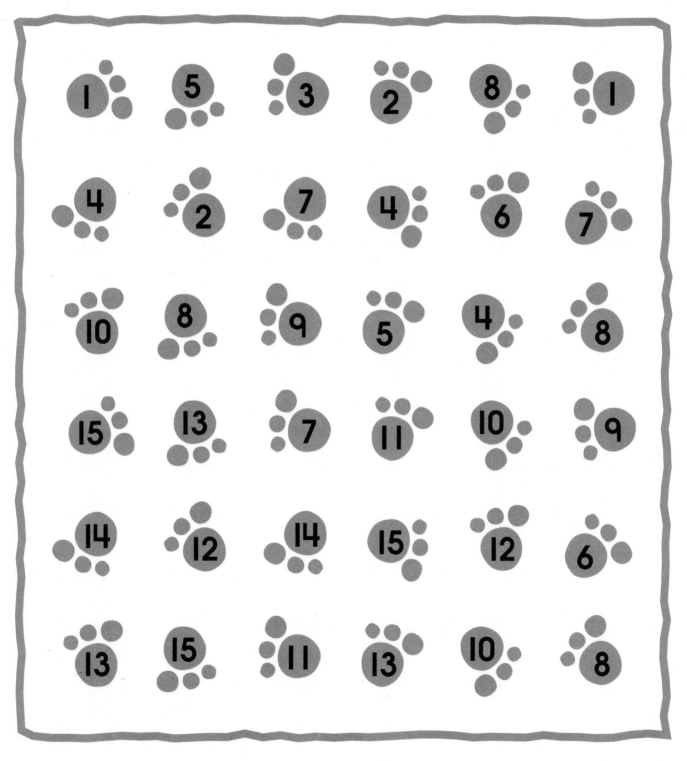

Number

Color the number. Color the word. Color the rest of the picture.

✏ **Trace** the number. **Trace** the word.

16   sixteen

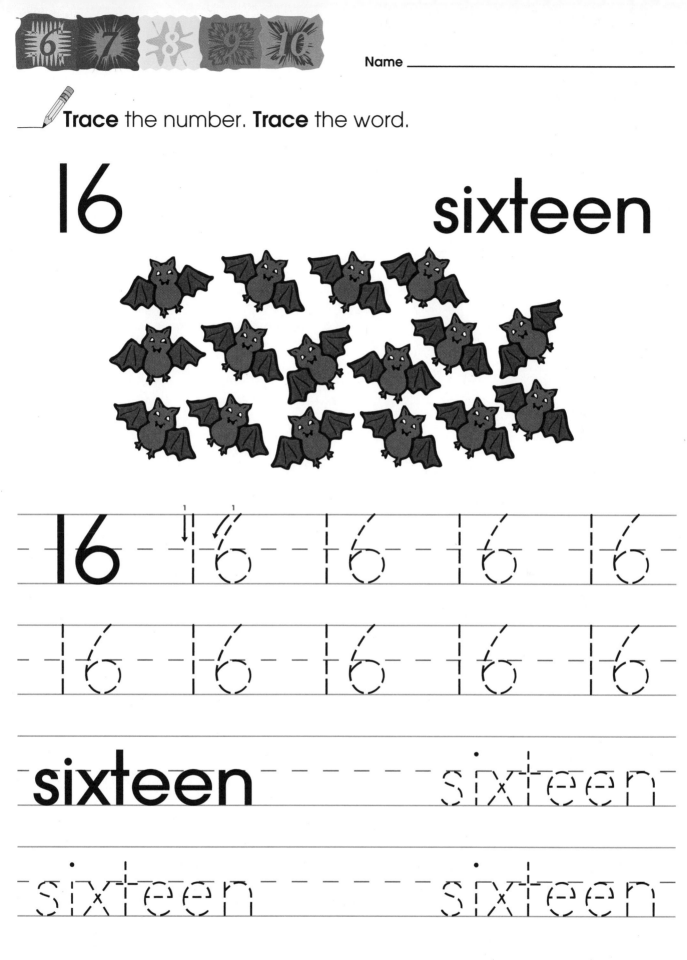

16   16   16   16   16

16   16   16   16   16

sixteen   sixteen

sixteen   sixteen

Now practice **writing** the number and the word by yourself on the lines below.

16

sixteen

Name _____

Draw 16 fish in the fish bowl! **Color** the picture.

Number

Color the number. Color the word. Color the rest of the picture.

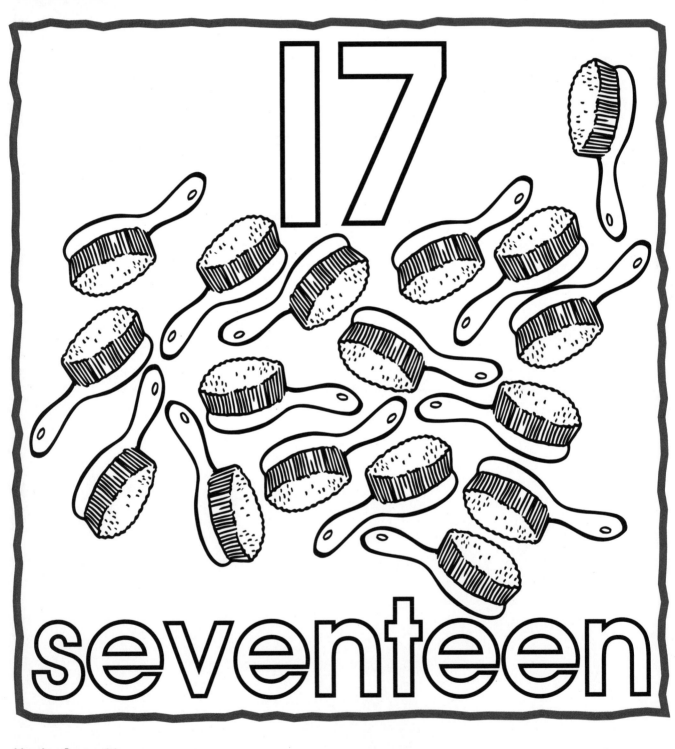

Name _____

✏️ **Trace** the number. **Trace** the word.

17   seventeen

17

17 17 17 17 17

17 17 17 17 17

seventeen seventeen

seventeen seventeen

Now practice **writing** the number and the word by yourself on the lines below.

17

seventeen

Name _____

Draw 17 birds in the tree. **Color** the picture.

Number

Color the number. **Color** the word. **Color** the rest of the picture.

Name _____

✏ **Trace** the number. **Trace** the word.

18

eighteen

18

18 18 18 18

18 18 18 18 18

eighteen eighteen

eighteen eighteen

Name _____

Now practice **writing** the number and the word by yourself on the lines below.

18

eighteen

Draw 18 ⭐s on the 🪨. **Color** the ⭐s.

Name _____

Number

Color the number. **Color** the word. **Color** the rest of the picture.

Number Recognition

Name _____

✏️ **Trace** the number. **Trace** the word.

19   nineteen

19   19   19   19   19

19   19   19   19   19

nineteen   nineteen

nineteen   nineteen

Number Recognition

Name _____

Now practice **writing** the number and the word by yourself on the lines below.

1 9

nineteen

Name _____

Draw 19 cookies in the cookie jar. **Color** the picture.

Number Recognition

141

Name _____

Number

20

Color the number. **Color** the word. **Color** the rest of the picture.

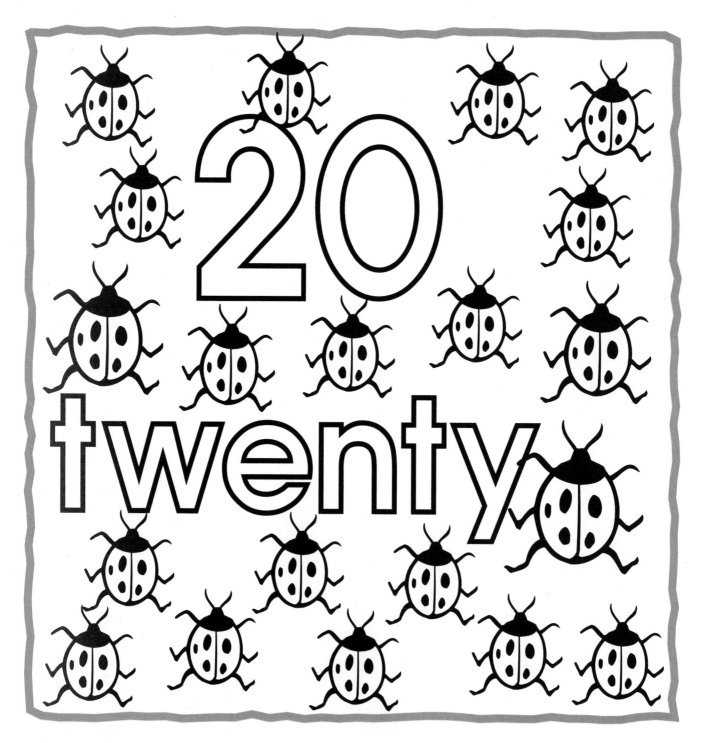

20

twenty

Number Recognition

Name _____

✏️ **Trace** the number. **Trace** the word.

20 twenty

20 ²⁰20 20 20 20

20 20 20 20 20 20

twenty twenty

twenty twenty

Number Recognition

Now practice **writing** the number and the word by yourself on the lines below.

20

twenty

Name _____

Draw 20 🚀s on the ◎. Color the 🚀s.

Name _____

Practice 1-20. 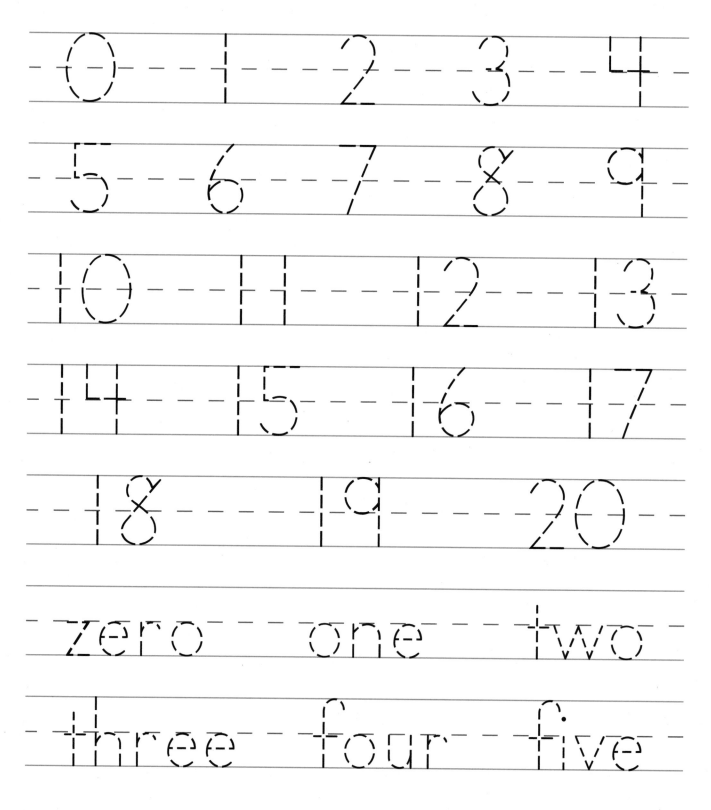Trace the numbers and the words.

0   1   2   3   4

5   6   7   8   9

10   11   12   13

14   15   16   17

18   19   20

zero   one   two

three   four   five

Name _____

Trace the numbers words.

six seven eight

nine ten eleven

twelve thirteen

fourteen

fifteen sixteen

seventeen eighteen

nineteen twenty

Review Numbers 0-20

Name _____

Connect the dots in order from **1-12**. **Color** the picture.

Name _____

Connect the dots in order from **0-20**. **Color** the picture.

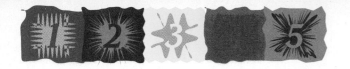

Name _____

Connect the dots in order from **1-20**. **Color** the surprise.

What is it?

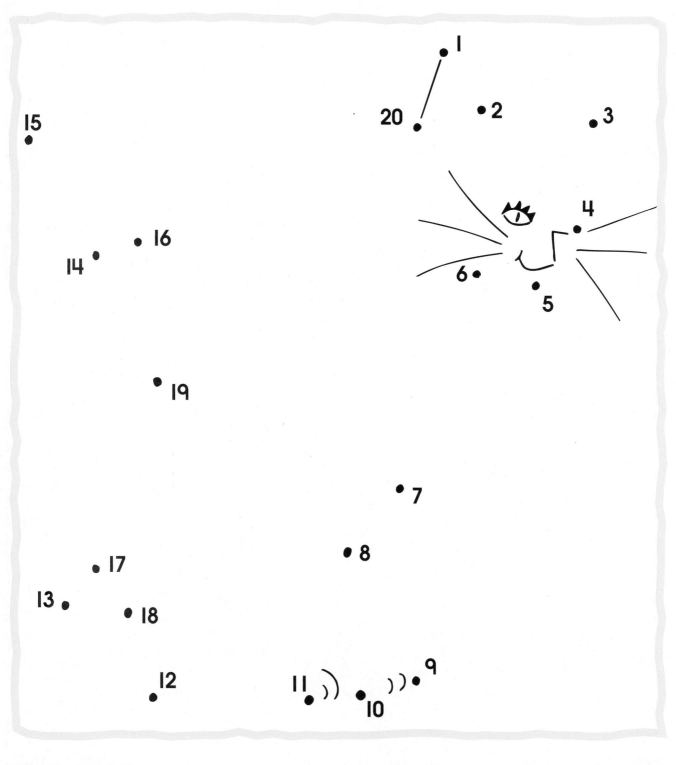

Name _____

Connect the numbers in order from **0-20** to help the kitten finds its home. **Color** the picture.

Name _____

Draw a line from the word to the correct number.

seven	1
two	8
five	3
nine	4
zero	7
six	5
four	6
one	2
three	0
eight	9

Color the train cars: 1 - red   2 - blue   3 - green   4 - yellow
5 - orange   6 - brown

Review Numbers 0-20

Name _____

Count the number of each thing in the picture. **Write** the number in the correct box.

Review Numbers 0–20

153

Name _____

Count the number of each thing in the picture. **Write** the number in the correct box.

Name _____

Count the cats in each bed. **Write** the correct number of cats in the box on each bed.

CONGRATULATIONS!

You know numbers **1-20**! **Color** this ribbon for everyone to see!

Place Value

Name _____

✏️ **Circle** sets of ten marbles. **Count** how many tens and ones. **Write** the number. ✏️

A.

tens	ones
1	4

14

B.

tens	ones

_____

C.

tens	ones

_____

D.

tens	ones

_____

E.

tens	ones

_____

F.

tens	ones

_____

G.

tens	ones

_____

H.

tens	ones

_____

Place Value Numbers to 100

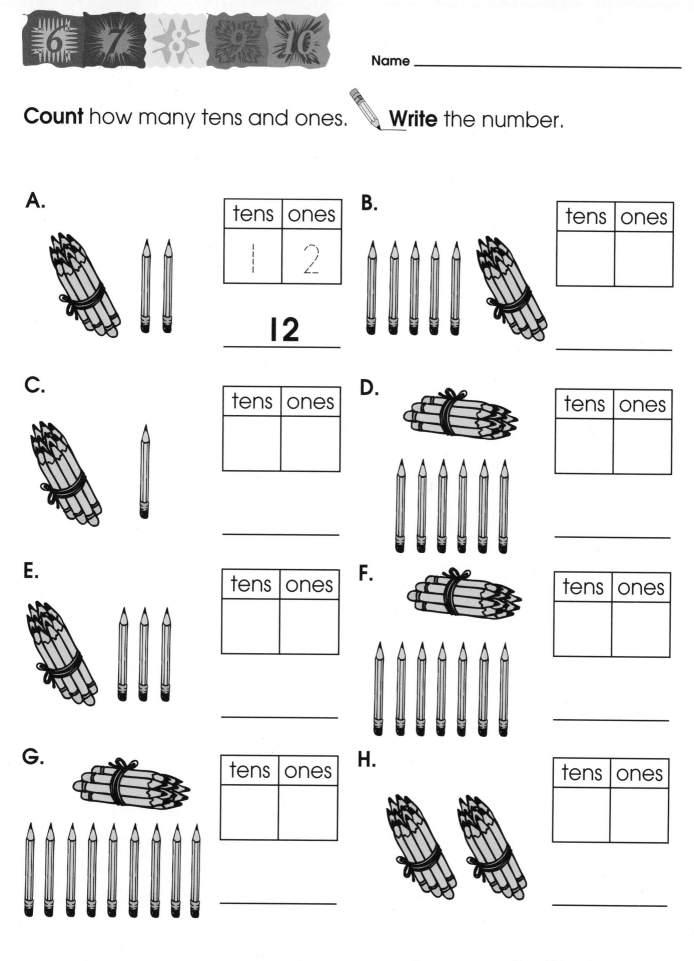

Count how many tens and ones. ✏ **Write** the number.

A.

tens	ones
1	2

12
_____

B.

tens	ones

_____

C.

tens	ones

_____

D.

tens	ones

_____

E.

tens	ones

_____

F.

tens	ones

_____

G.

tens	ones

_____

H.

tens	ones

_____

Use the numbers on the left of the charts to **write** in the ones place to see how numbers **20–29** are made. The number in the tens place stays the same for all ten numbers.

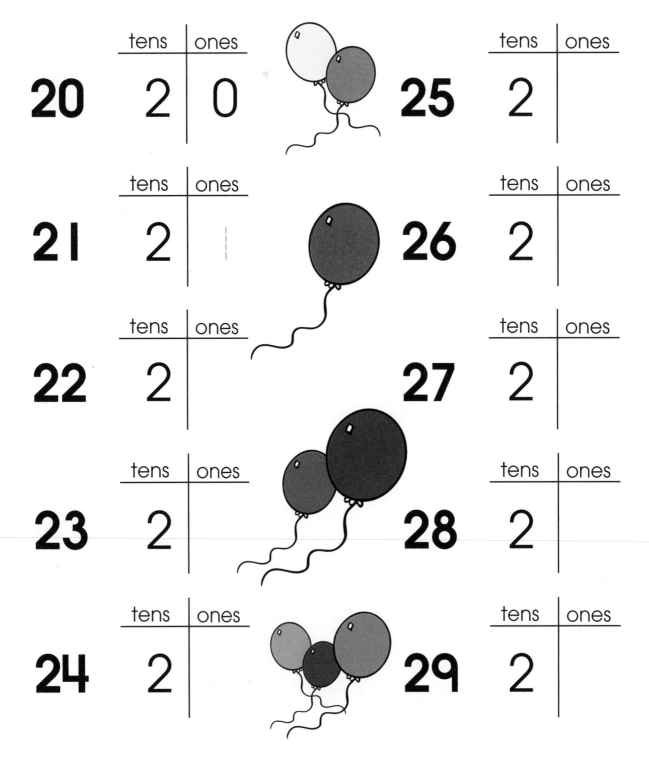

	tens	ones
20	2	0

	tens	ones
21	2	

	tens	ones
22	2	

	tens	ones
23	2	

	tens	ones
24	2	

	tens	ones
25	2	

	tens	ones
26	2	

	tens	ones
27	2	

	tens	ones
28	2	

	tens	ones
29	2	

Place Value Numbers to 100

Name _____

Use the numbers on the left of the charts to **write** in the ones place to see how numbers **30–39** are made. The number in the tens place stays the same for all ten numbers.

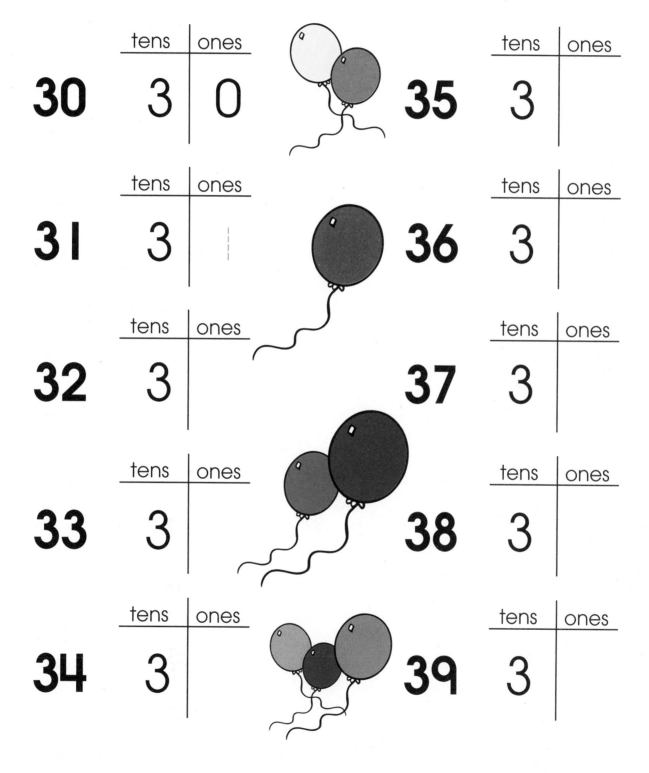

	tens	ones
30	3	0

	tens	ones
31	3	

	tens	ones
32	3	

	tens	ones
33	3	

	tens	ones
34	3	

	tens	ones
35	3	

	tens	ones
36	3	

	tens	ones
37	3	

	tens	ones
38	3	

	tens	ones
39	3	

Place Value Numbers to 100

Use the numbers on the left of the charts to **write** in the ones place to see how numbers **40–49** are made. The number in the tens place stays the same for all ten numbers.

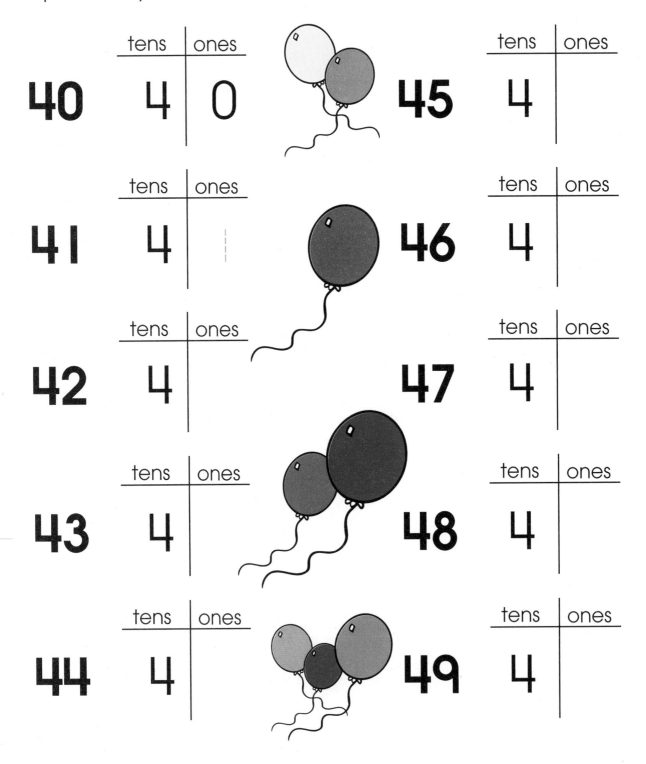

	tens	ones
40	4	0

	tens	ones
41	4	

	tens	ones
42	4	

	tens	ones
43	4	

	tens	ones
44	4	

	tens	ones
45	4	

	tens	ones
46	4	

	tens	ones
47	4	

	tens	ones
48	4	

	tens	ones
49	4	

Count the numbers from **1–50**.

1	2	3	4	5
6	7	8	9	10
11	12	13	14	15
16	17	18	19	20
21	22	23	24	25
26	27	28	29	30
31	32	33	34	35
36	37	38	39	40
41	42	43	44	45
46	47	48	49	50

Place Value Numbers to 100

Name _____

Connect the dots in order from **1-50**. **Color** the creature.

What is it?

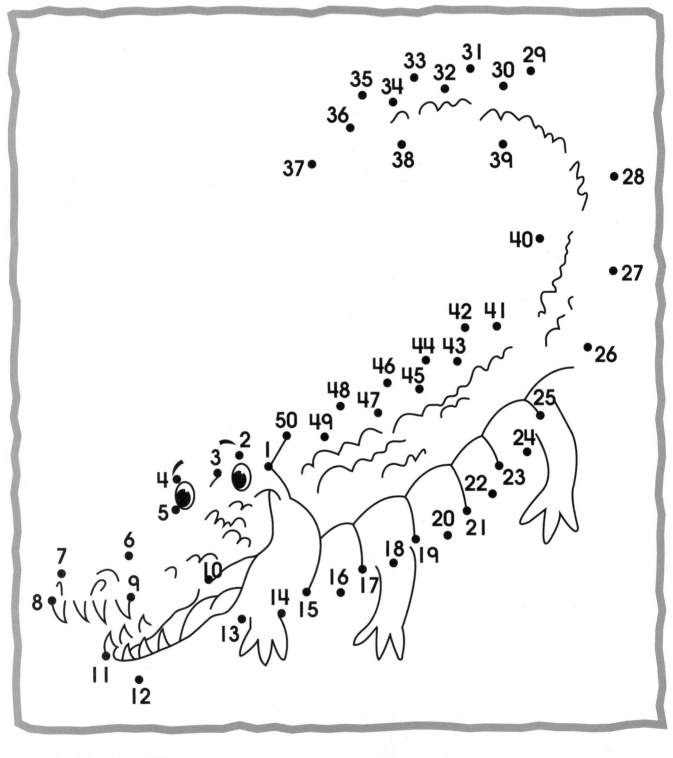

Name _____

Use the numbers on the left of the charts to **write** in the ones place to see how numbers **50–59** are made. The number in the tens place stays the same for all ten numbers.

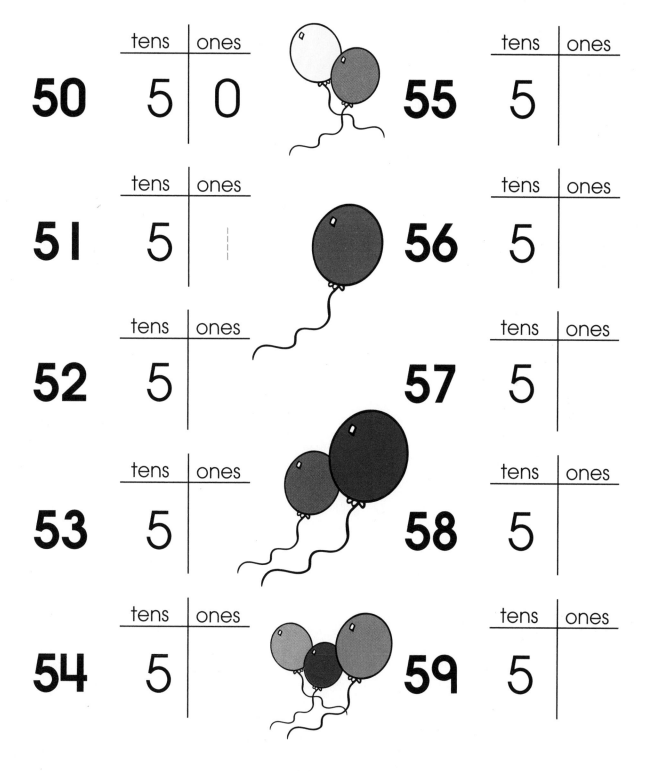

	tens	ones
50	5	0

	tens	ones
51	5	

	tens	ones
52	5	

	tens	ones
53	5	

	tens	ones
54	5	

	tens	ones
55	5	

	tens	ones
56	5	

	tens	ones
57	5	

	tens	ones
58	5	

	tens	ones
59	5	

Use the numbers on the left of the charts to **write** in the ones place to see how numbers **60–69** are made. The number in the tens place stays the same for all ten numbers.

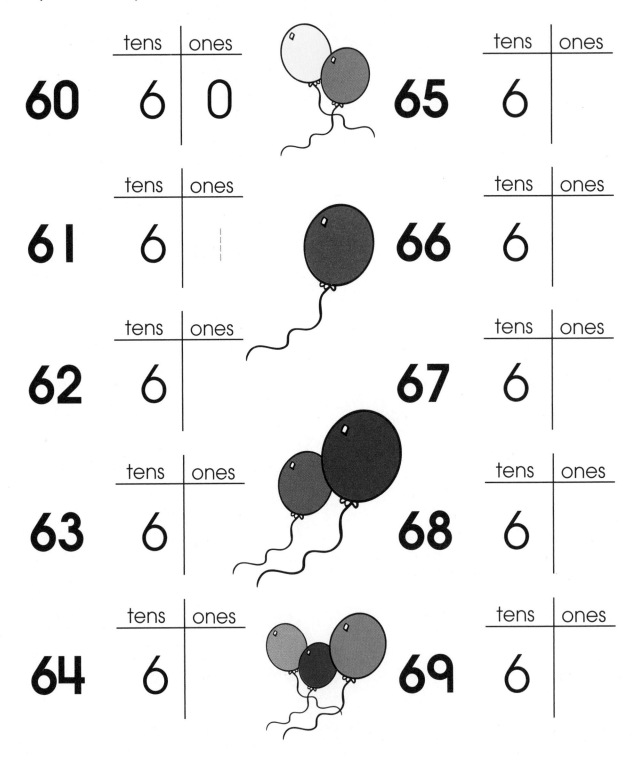

	tens	ones
60	6	0

	tens	ones
61	6	

	tens	ones
62	6	

	tens	ones
63	6	

	tens	ones
64	6	

	tens	ones
65	6	

	tens	ones
66	6	

	tens	ones
67	6	

	tens	ones
68	6	

	tens	ones
69	6	

Place Value Numbers to 100

Name _____

Use the numbers on the left of the charts to **write** in the ones place to see how numbers **70–79** are made. The number in the tens place stays the same for all ten numbers.

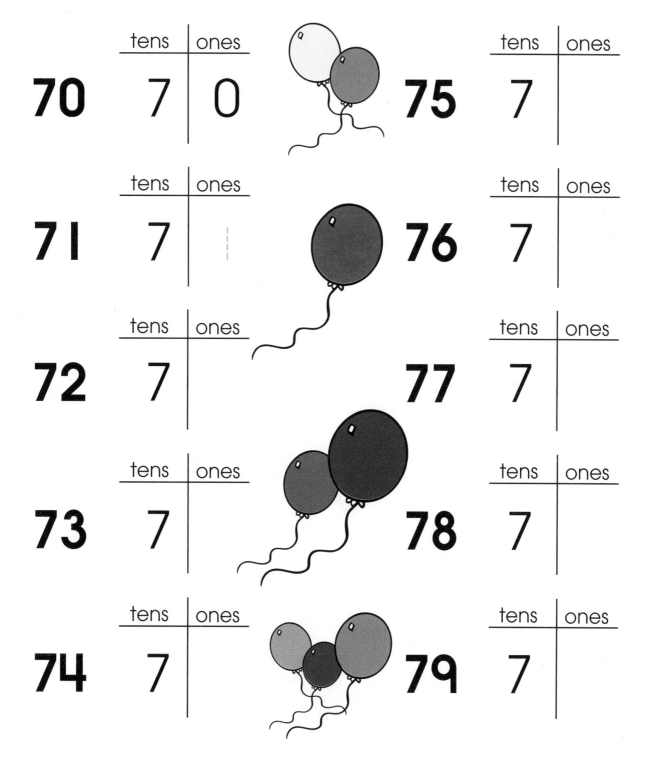

	tens	ones
70	7	0

	tens	ones
75	7	

	tens	ones
71	7	

	tens	ones
76	7	

	tens	ones
72	7	

	tens	ones
77	7	

	tens	ones
73	7	

	tens	ones
78	7	

	tens	ones
74	7	

	tens	ones
79	7	

Name _____

✏️ Use the numbers on the left of the charts to **write** in the ones place to see how numbers **80-89** are made. The number in the tens place stays the same for all ten numbers.

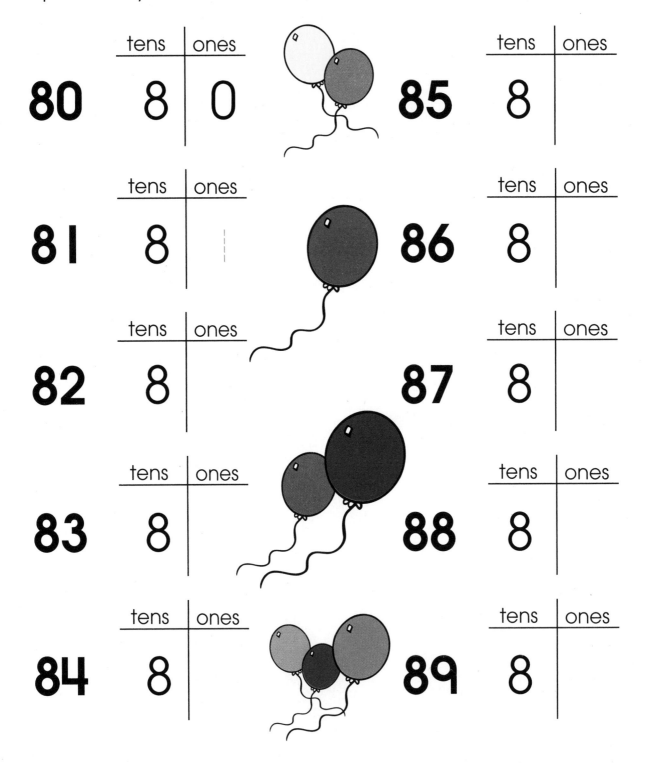

	tens	ones
80	8	0

	tens	ones
81	8	

	tens	ones
82	8	

	tens	ones
83	8	

	tens	ones
84	8	

	tens	ones
85	8	

	tens	ones
86	8	

	tens	ones
87	8	

	tens	ones
88	8	

	tens	ones
89	8	

Place Value Numbers to 100

Name _____

Use the numbers on the left of the charts to **write** in the ones place to see how numbers **90-99** are made. The number in the tens place stays the same for all ten numbers.

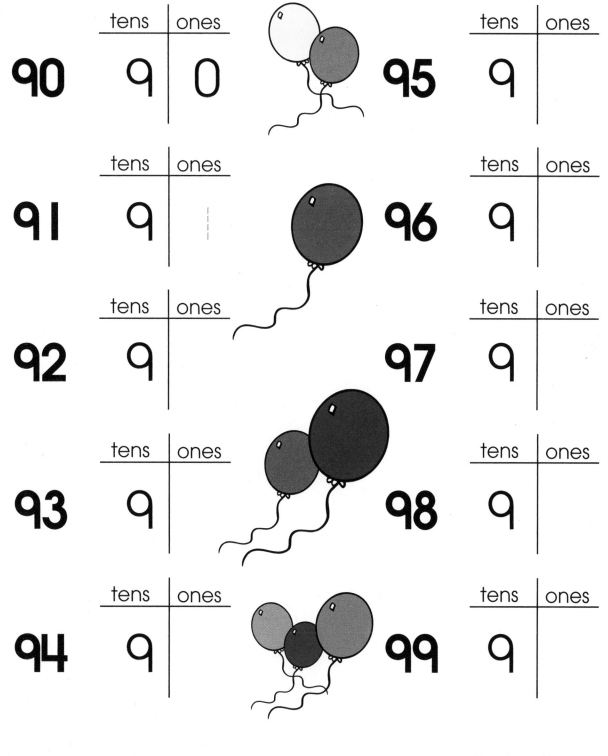

90

tens	ones
9	0

95

tens	ones
9	

91

tens	ones
9	

96

tens	ones
9	

92

tens	ones
9	

97

tens	ones
9	

93

tens	ones
9	

98

tens	ones
9	

94

tens	ones
9	

99

tens	ones
9	

Place Value Numbers to 100

Name _____

Use the place value chart to build each number. ✏ **Write** the numbers in the table.

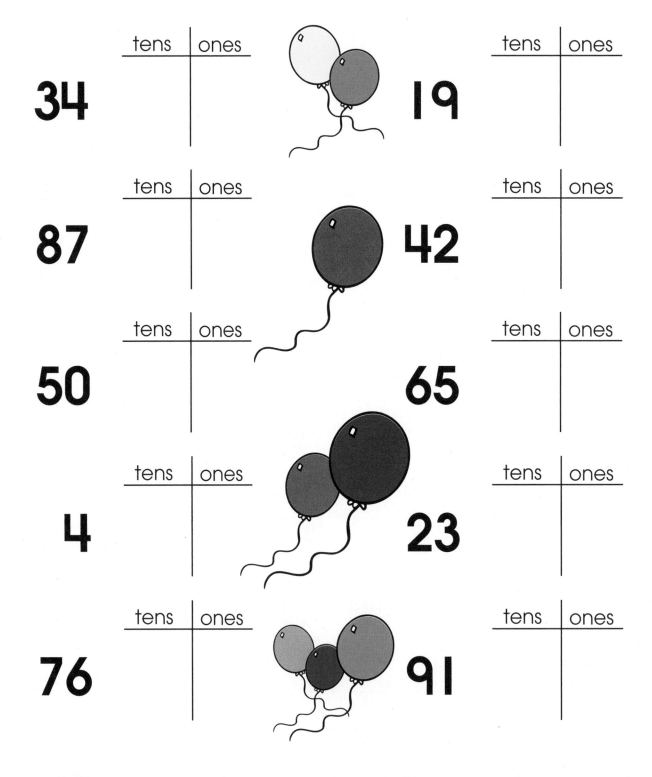

tens	ones

34

tens	ones

19

tens	ones

87

tens	ones

42

tens	ones

50

tens	ones

65

tens	ones

4

tens	ones

23

tens	ones

76

tens	ones

91

Place Value Numbers to 100

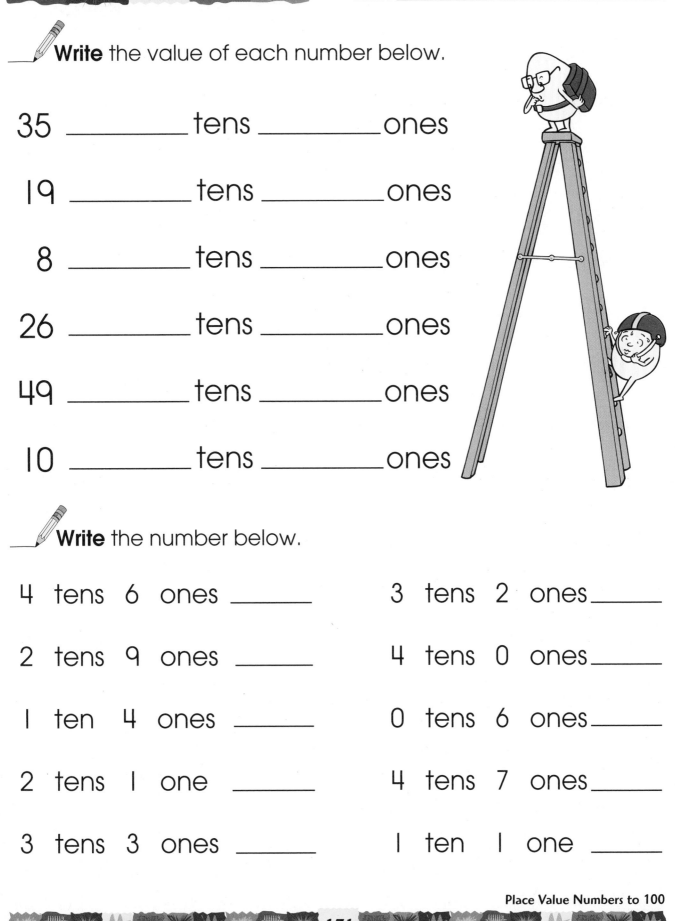

Name _____

✏️ **Write** the value of each number below.

35 _____ tens _____ ones

19 _____ tens _____ ones

8 _____ tens _____ ones

26 _____ tens _____ ones

49 _____ tens _____ ones

10 _____ tens _____ ones

✏️ **Write** the number below.

4 tens 6 ones _____   3 tens 2 ones _____

2 tens 9 ones _____   4 tens 0 ones _____

1 ten 4 ones _____   0 tens 6 ones _____

2 tens 1 one _____   4 tens 7 ones _____

3 tens 3 ones _____   1 ten 1 one _____

Add the ones and tens. **Write** the answer on the blank.

Example:

$+$ = 33

3 tens $+$ **3 ones** = **33**

7 tens + 5 ones = _____

2 tens + 3 ones = _____

5 tens + 2 ones = _____

5 tens + 4 ones = _____

9 tens + 5 ones = _____

4 tens + 0 ones = _____

8 tens + 1 one = _____

1 ten + 1 one = _____

6 tens + 3 ones = _____

3 tens + 7 ones = _____

Draw a line to the correct number.

6 tens + 7 ones   73

4 tens + 2 ones   67

8 tens + 0 ones   51

7 tens + 3 ones   80

5 tens + 1 one   42

Name _____

Count the numbers from **1-100**.

1	2	3	4	5	6	7	8	9	10
11	12	13	14	15	16	17	18	19	20
21	22	23	24	25	26	27	28	29	30
31	32	33	34	35	36	37	38	39	40
41	42	43	44	45	46	47	48	49	50
51	52	53	54	55	56	57	58	59	60
61	62	63	64	65	66	67	68	69	70
71	72	73	74	75	76	77	78	79	80
81	82	83	84	85	86	87	88	89	90
91	92	93	94	95	96	97	98	99	100

Place Value Numbers to 100

Name _____

Color the ball **red** if the number is **30-39**. **Color** the ball **purple** if the number is **40-49**. **Color** the ball **blue** if the number is **50-59**. **Color** the ball **green** if the number is **60-69**.

Connect the dots in order from **1-75**. **Color** the animal.

What is it?

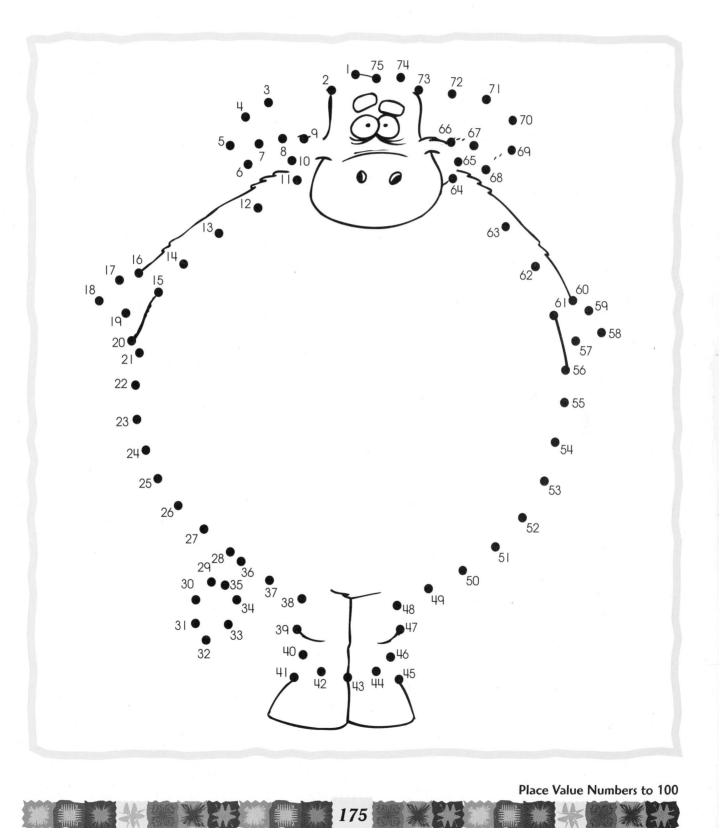

Name _____

Color the bubble **red** if the number is **1-25**. Color the bubble **orange** if the number is **26-50**. Color the bubble **yellow** if the number is **51-75**. Color the bubble **blue** if the number is **76-100**.

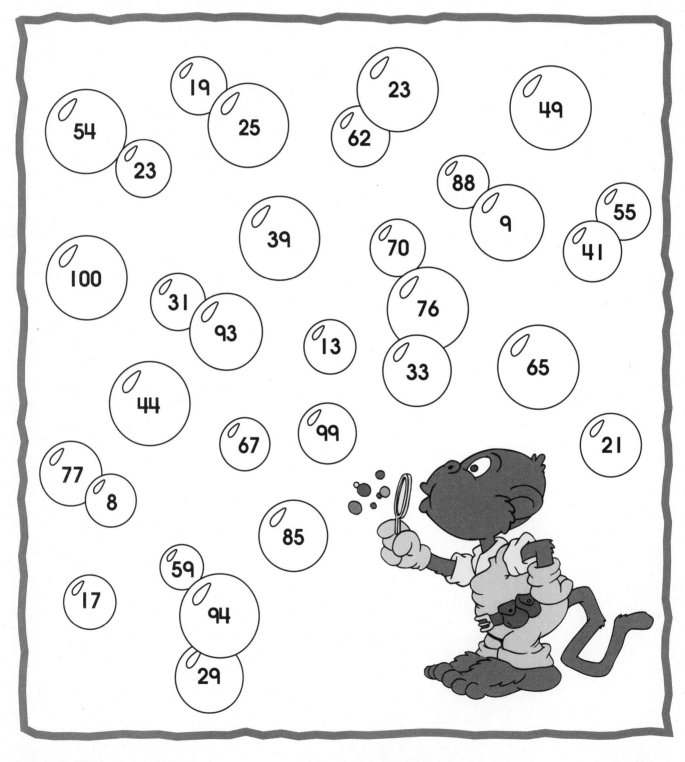

Place Value Numbers to 100

Counting

Name _____

This is how to count by **2's**. Begin with the number **2**. If you add **2**, you get **4**. If you add **2** more, you get **6**, and so on. Use the number line to help you.

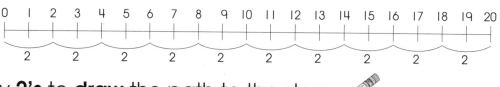

Count by **2's** to **draw** the path to the store. ✏️

Count by **2's**. **Write** the numbers to **30** in the water drops. Begin at the top of the slide and go down.

Name _____

Count by **2's.** ✏ **Write** the numbers on the notes.

Use the letters on the notes to find out the name of the song the frog is singing.

"   ,
___ ___ ___ ___   ___ ___
 28   22   2   2   4   22

,
___ ___ ___ ___ ___ ___ ___ ___
 16   44   26   36   38   6   10   18

___ ___ ___ ___ ___   ___ ___ ___
 44   26   40   10   8   48   32   22
                                      "
___ ___ ___ ___ ___ ___ ___ ___ '
 4   36   16   38   30   50   44   8

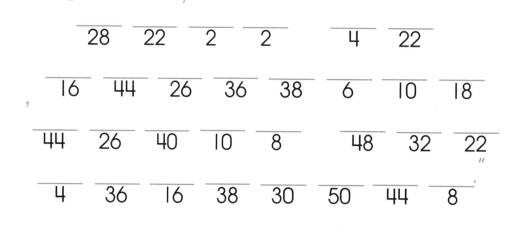

This is how to count by **5's**. Begin with the number **5**. If you add **5**, you get **10**. If you add **5** more, you get **15**, and so on. Use the number line to help you.

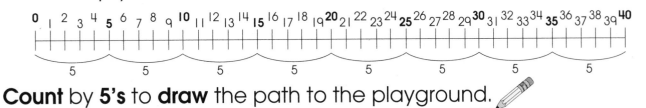

Count by **5's** to **draw** the path to the playground.

Name _____

Count by **2's**. ✏ **Trace** then **write** the numbers below.

2		6							

Count by **5's**. ✏ **Trace** then **write** the numbers below.

5		15							

Count by **2's**.
Connect the dots.
Color the picture.

What is it?

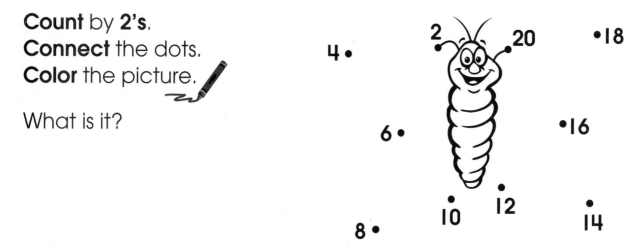

Count by **5's**. **Connect** the dots.
Color the picture.

What is it?

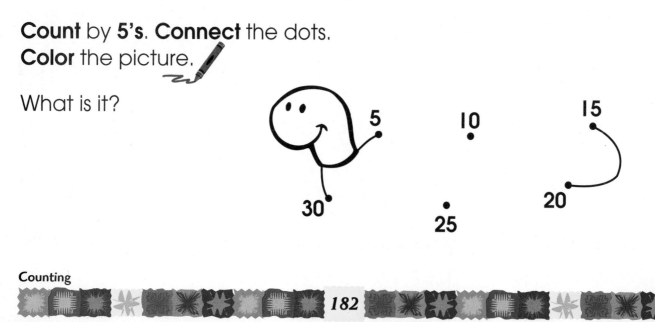

Name _____

Find out what holds something good! **Count** by **5's** to connect the dots. **Color** the picture.

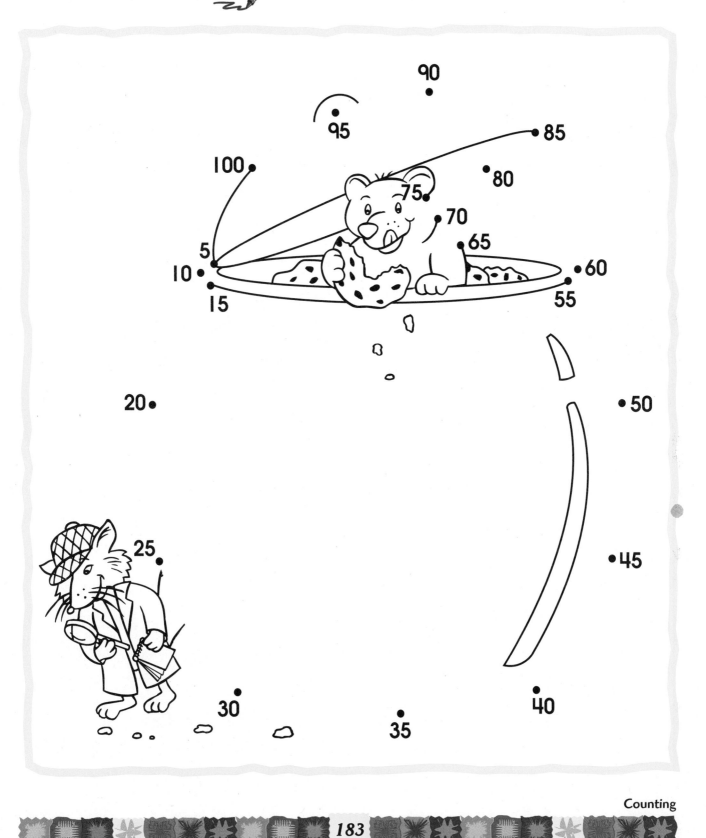

Name _____

Help the bird count the twigs needed to build its nest. **Count** by **5's**.
Write the numbers in the box.

Name _____

This is how to count by **10's**. Begin with the number **10**. If you add **10**, you get **20**. If you add **10** more, you get **30**, and so on. Use the number line to help you.

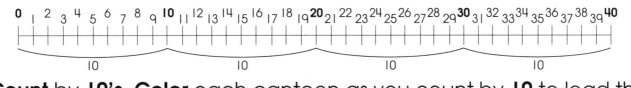

Count by **10's**. **Color** each canteen as you count by **10** to lead the camel to the watering hole.

Count by **5's**.
Draw triangles around each number in the box.

1	2	3	4	5	6	7	8	9	10
11	12	13	14	15	16	17	18	19	20
21	22	23	24	25	26	27	28	29	30
31	32	33	34	35	36	37	38	39	40
41	42	43	44	45	46	47	48	49	50

Count by **5's**.

5   10   ____   ____   ____   ____   ____   ____

____   ____

Count by **10's**.
Draw boxes around each number in the box.

1	2	3	4	5	6	7	8	9	10
11	12	13	14	15	16	17	18	19	20
21	22	23	24	25	26	27	28	29	30
31	32	33	34	35	36	37	38	39	40
41	42	43	44	45	46	47	48	49	50

Count by **10's**.

10   ____   ____   ____   ____

Counting

Name _____

Count by **10's** to complete each row. **Write** the numbers below each basket.

20 ___ ___ ___ ___

50 ___ ___ ___ ___

40 ___ ___ ___ ___

30 ___ ___ ___ ___

Counting

Name _____

✏ **Write** the missing numbers.

Count by 2's:

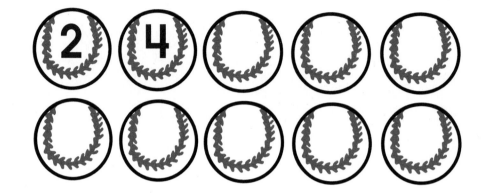

Count by 5's:

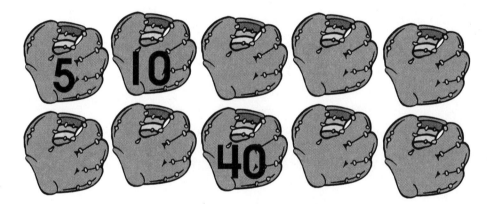

Count by 10's:

Name _____

Count by **2's**, **5's**, and **10's** to find the "critter count." **Write** the number on the line beside each row.

Each worm = **2**. **Count** by **2's** to find the total.

= _____

= _____

Each turtle = **5**. **Count** by **5's** to find the total.

= _____

= _____

Each ladybug = **10**. **Count** by **10's** to find the total.

= _____

= _____

Counting

Name _____

Another way of counting is **first** for 1, **second** for **2**, **third** for **3**, and so on. These are called **ordinal numbers**.

Color the **second** ball **brown**.

Color the **sixth** ball yellow.

Color the **fourth** ball orange.

Color the **first** ball **black**.

Color the **fifth** ball green.

Color the **seventh** ball purple.

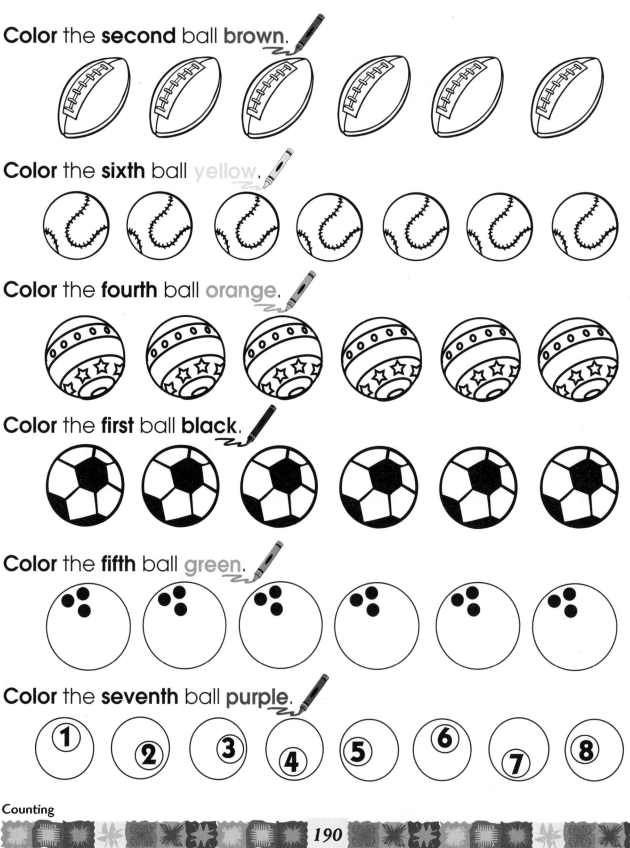

Counting

Name _____

Next to each ordinal number, **write** the color of the car in that position.

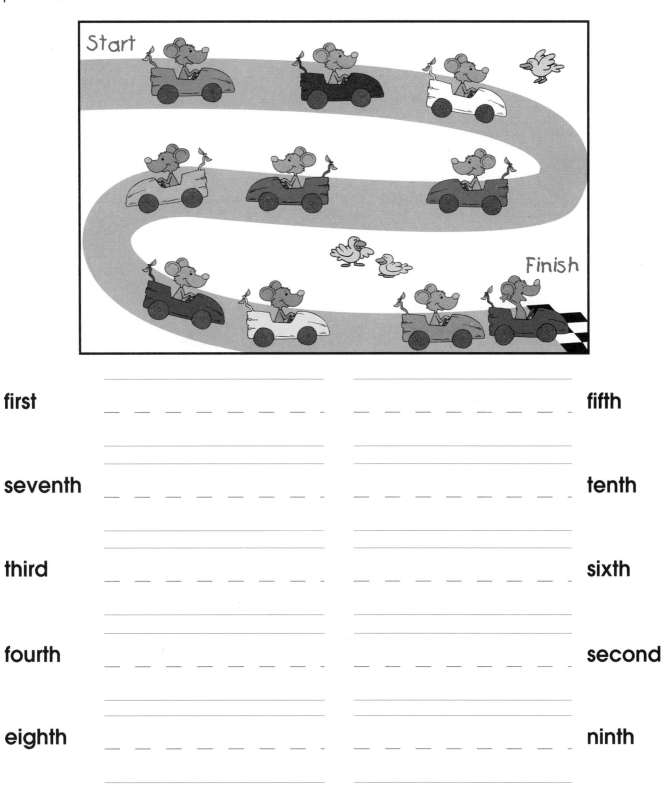

first _ _ _ _ _ _ _ _ _ _ _ _ _ _ _ _   fifth

seventh _ _ _ _ _ _ _ _ _ _ _ _   tenth

third _ _ _ _ _ _ _ _ _ _ _ _ _ _   sixth

fourth _ _ _ _ _ _ _ _ _ _ _ _   second

eighth _ _ _ _ _ _ _ _ _ _ _ _   ninth

Counting

Name _____

Write each word on the correct line to put the words in order.

| second | fifth | seventh | first | tenth |
| third | eighth | sixth | fourth | ninth |

1. _____   6. _____

2. _____   7. _____

3. _____   8. _____

4. _____   9. _____

5. _____   10. _____

Which picture is circled in each row? **Underline** the word that tells the correct number.

third   fourth

fourth   sixth

first   ninth

third   fifth

fifth   sixth

second   third

Comparing

Name _____

✏ **Circle** the correct numbers in each box.

Numbers **less** than **3**

| 1 | 2 | 3 | 4 | 5 | 6 | 7 | 8 | 9 | 10 | 11 | 12 |

Numbers **greater** than **10**

| 1 | 2 | 3 | 4 | 5 | 6 | 7 | 8 | 9 | 10 | 11 | 12 |

Numbers **equal** to **7**

| 1 | 2 | 3 | 4 | 5 | 6 | 7 | 8 | 9 | 10 | 11 | 12 |

Numbers **greater** than **2**

| 1 | 2 | 3 | 4 | 5 | 6 | 7 | 8 | 9 | 10 | 11 | 12 |

Numbers **less** than **10**

| 1 | 2 | 3 | 4 | 5 | 6 | 7 | 8 | 9 | 10 | 11 | 12 |

Numbers **greater** than **7**

| 1 | 2 | 3 | 4 | 5 | 6 | 7 | 8 | 9 | 10 | 11 | 12 |

Comparing

Name _____

In each shape, **circle** the smallest number. **Draw** a square around the largest number.

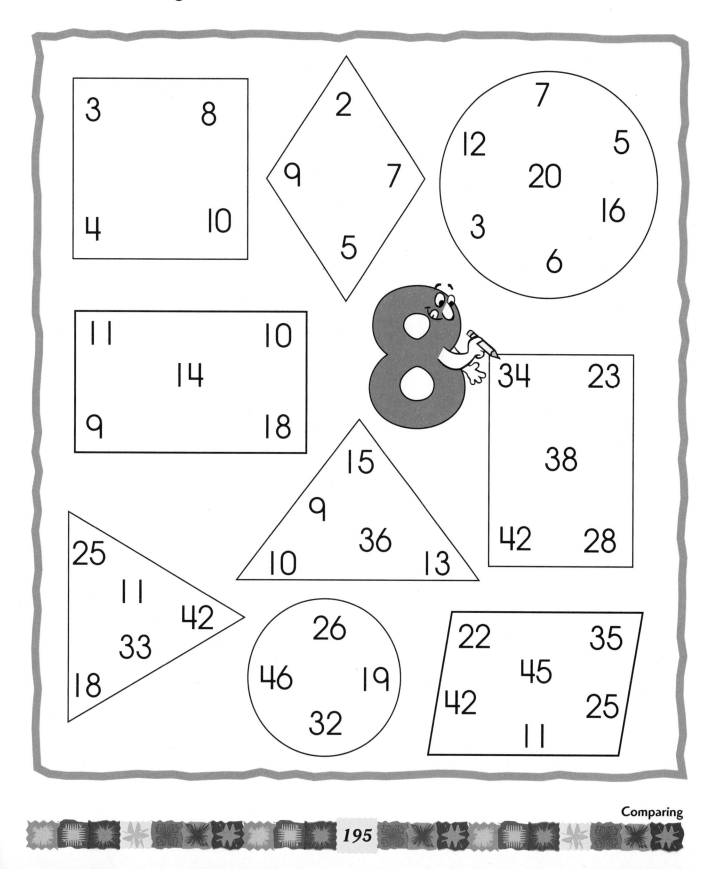

Name _____

The symbol **>** means the first number is **greater than** the second number. The symbol **<** means the first number is **less than** the second number.

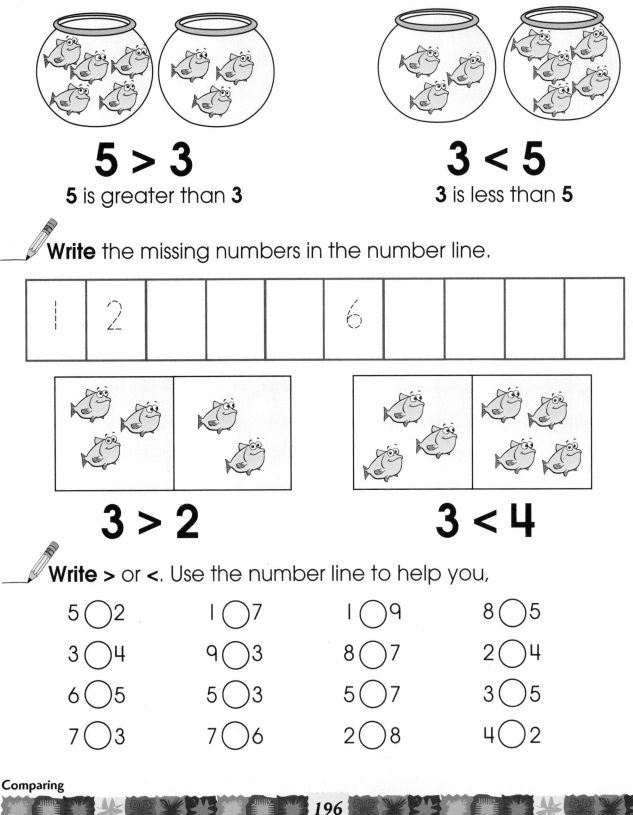

5 > 3
5 is greater than **3**

3 < 5
3 is less than **5**

✏️ **Write** the missing numbers in the number line.

1	2				6				

3 > 2

3 < 4

✏️ **Write >** or **<**. Use the number line to help you,

5 ◯ 2   1 ◯ 7   1 ◯ 9   8 ◯ 5

3 ◯ 4   9 ◯ 3   8 ◯ 7   2 ◯ 4

6 ◯ 5   5 ◯ 3   5 ◯ 7   3 ◯ 5

7 ◯ 3   7 ◯ 6   2 ◯ 8   4 ◯ 2

Comparing

Name _____

✏ **Circle** the numbers in each line that make the sentence correct.

3 | < | 0 1 2 3 4 5 6 7 8 9 10

7 | > | 0 1 2 3 4 5 6 7 8 9 10

4 | = | 0 1 2 3 4 5 6 7 8 9 10

8 | < | 0 1 2 3 4 5 6 7 8 9 10

2 | > | 0 1 2 3 4 5 6 7 8 9 10

5 | < | 0 1 2 3 4 5 6 7 8 9 10

10 | > | 0 1 2 3 4 5 6 7 8 9 10

1 | > | 9 4 0

0 | < | 2 7 10

9 | = | 4 8 9

Write < or > in each circle. Make sure the "mouth" is open toward the greater number.

36 ◯ 49   35 ◯ 53

20 ◯ 18   74 ◯ 21

53 ◯ 76   68 ◯ 80

29 ◯ 26   45 ◯ 19

90 ◯ 89   70 ◯ 67

Name _____

Compare the numbers. **Write** the answer to each question on the line.

Which is **greater**? _____

How much **greater**? _____

Which is **greater**? _____

How much **greater**? _____

Which is **less**? _____

How much **less**? _____

Which is **less**? _____

How much **less**? _____

Which is **greater**? _____

How much **greater**? _____

Who has the **most**? **Circle** the correct answer.

1. Traci has **3** s.

   Bob has **4** s.

   Bill has **5** s.

   Who has the **most** s?

   Traci   Bob   Bill

2. Pam has **7** s.

   Joe has **5** s.

   Jane has **6** s.

   Who has the **most** s?

   Pam   Joe   Jane

3. Jennifer has **23** s.

   Sandy has **19** s.

   Jack has **25** s.

   Who has the **most** s?

   Jennifer   Sandy   Jack

4. Ali has **19** s.

   Burt has **18** s.

   Brent has **17** s.

   Who has the **most** s?

   Ali   Burt   Brent

5. The boys have **14** s.

   The girls have **16** s.

   The teachers have **17** s.

   Who has the **most** s?

   boys   girls   teachers

6. Rose has **12** s.

   Betsy has **11** s.

   Leslie has **13** s.

   Who has the **most** s?

   Rose   Betsy   Leslie

Who has the **fewest**? Circle the correct answer.

1. Pat had **4** ⚽s.

   Charles had **3** ⚽s.

   Andrea had **5** ⚽s.

   Who had the **fewest** number

   of ⚽s?

   Pat   Charles   Andrea

2. Jeff has **5** 🏀s.

   John has **4** 🏀s.

   Bill has **6** 🏀s.

   Who has the **fewest** number

   of 🏀s?

   Jeff   John   Bill

3. Jane has **7** 🎾s.

   Susan has **9** 🎾s.

   Fred has **8** 🎾s.

   Who has the **fewest** number

   of 🎾s?

   Jane   Susan   Fred

4. Charles bought **12** ⚪s.

   Rose bought **6** ⚪s.

   Dawn bought **24** ⚪s.

   Who bought the **fewest**

   number of ⚪s?

   Charles   Rose   Dawn

5. John had **9** 🏈s.

   Jack had **8** 🏈s.

   Mark had **7** 🏈s.

   Who had the **fewest** number

   of 🏈s?

   John   Jack   Mark

6. Edith bought **12** ⚾s.

   Michelle bought **16** ⚾s.

   Marty bought **13** ⚾s.

   Who bought the **fewest**

   number of ⚾s?

   Edith   Michelle   Marty

Comparing

Addition and Subtraction

Count the number in each group and **write** the number on the line. Then, **add** the groups together and **write** the sum.

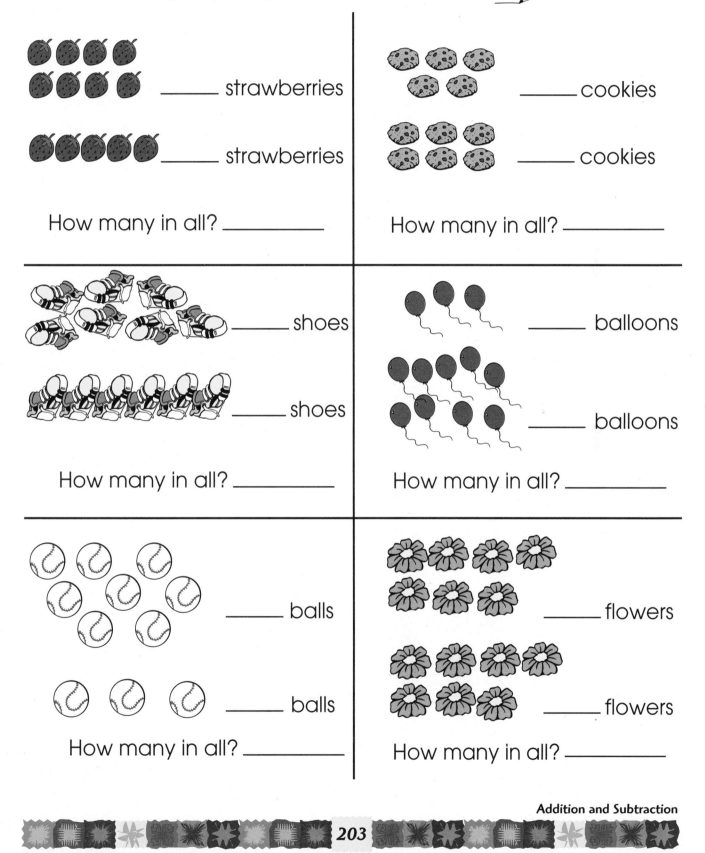

_____ strawberries

_____ strawberries

How many in all? _____

_____ cookies

_____ cookies

How many in all? _____

_____ shoes

_____ shoes

How many in all? _____

_____ balloons

_____ balloons

How many in all? _____

_____ balls

_____ balls

How many in all? _____

_____ flowers

_____ flowers

How many in all? _____

Addition and Subtraction

Name _____

Look at the pictures. **Write** the answer to each addition sentence. The first one is done for you.

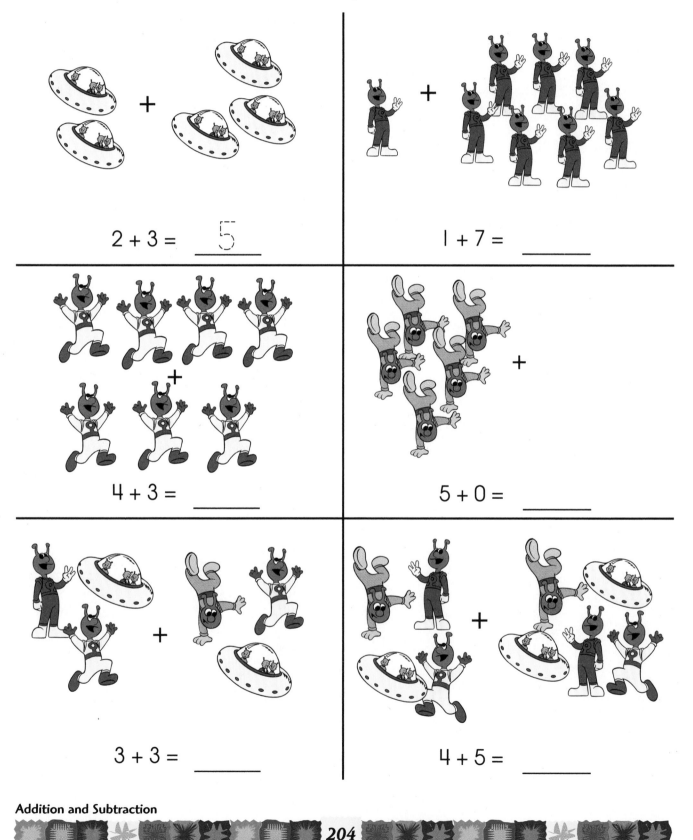

2 + 3 = __5__

1 + 7 = _____

4 + 3 = _____

5 + 0 = _____

3 + 3 = _____

4 + 5 = _____

Addition and Subtraction

Name _____

Look at the pictures. Complete the addition sentence. ✏ **Write** your answer in the doghouse.

2 + 6 =

7 + 3 =

6 + 1 =

4 + 5 =

6 + 2 =

7 + 2 =

Name _____

Circle the picture that matches the addition sentence.

1 + 2 = 3	3 + 2 = 5
2 + 4 = 6	3 + 3 = 6
3 + 4 = 7	1 + 6 = 7

Name _____

Draw the missing pictures. **Write** the answer to each addition sentence.

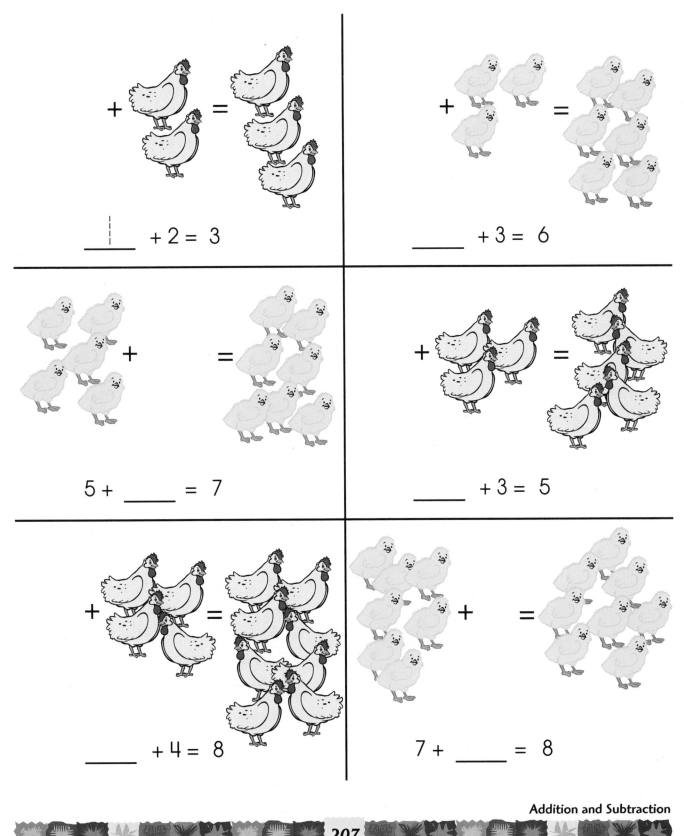

__1__ + 2 = 3

_____ + 3 = 6

5 + _____ = 7

_____ + 3 = 5

_____ + 4 = 8

7 + _____ = 8

Addition and Subtraction

Name _____

Add to find each sum.

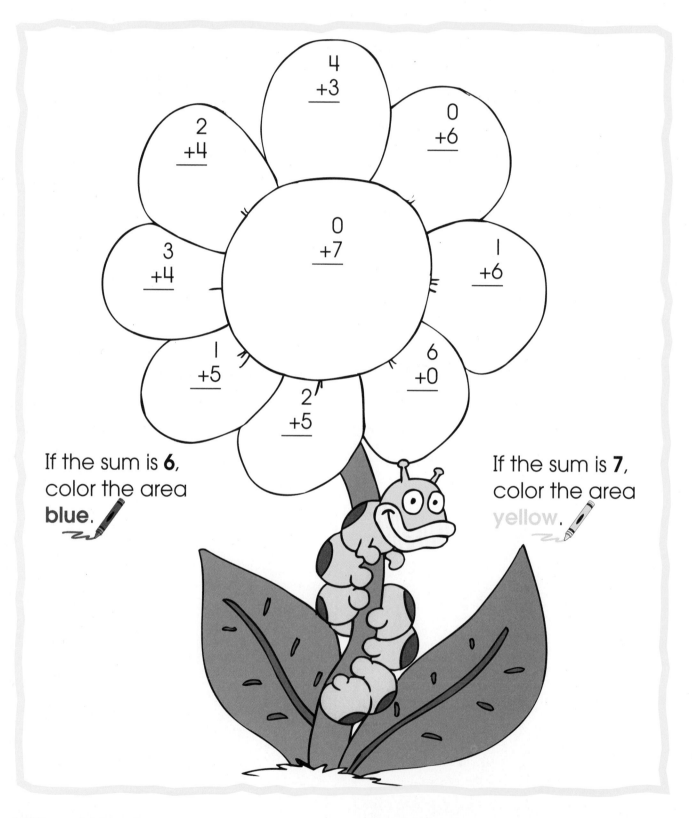

If the sum is **6**, color the area **blue**.

If the sum is **7**, color the area yellow.

Addition and Subtraction

Name _____

Add to find the sums. Use the code to **color** the picture.

1 — white   2 — yellow   3 — orange   4 — purple   5 — red
6 — pink   7 — gray   8 — brown   9 — green   10 — blue

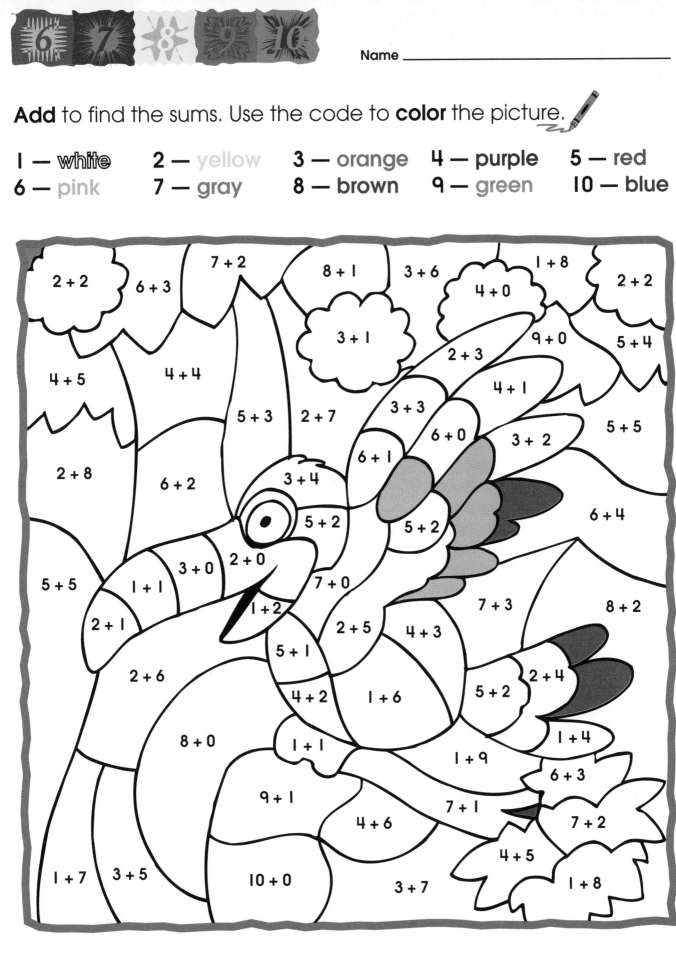

Name _____

Add to find each sum. Connect the dots in order. Use the sums and letters from the boxes to answer the riddle.

G 5 + 3	A 6 + 6	T 2 + 2	W 7 + 6	C 3 + 2
L 8 + 8	R 7 + 8	Y 5 + 5	U 4 + 3	E 9 + 9
N 2 + 9	O 5 + 4	P 9 + 8	I 6 + 8	E 1 + 2

Riddle: What do you get when you cross an eel and a goat?

$$\overline{10}\ \overline{9}\ \overline{7}\ \ \ \overline{13}\ \overline{14}\ \overline{16}\ \overline{16}$$

$$\overline{8}\ \overline{18}\ \overline{4}\ \ \ \overline{12}\ \overline{11}$$

$$\overline{3}\ \overline{16}\ \overline{18}\ \overline{5}\ \overline{4}\ \overline{15}\ \overline{14}\ \overline{5}$$

$$\overline{5}\ \overline{12}\ \overline{11}$$

$$\overline{9}\ \overline{17}\ \overline{18}\ \overline{11}\ \overline{18}\ \overline{15}$$

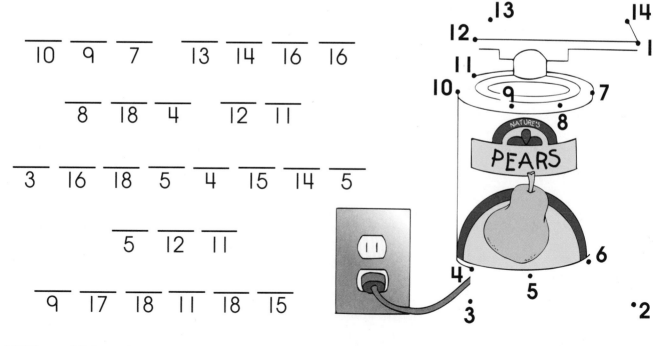

Name _____

Count the objects and fill in the blanks. Then, switch the numbers and **write** another addition sentence. The first one is done for you.

Example:

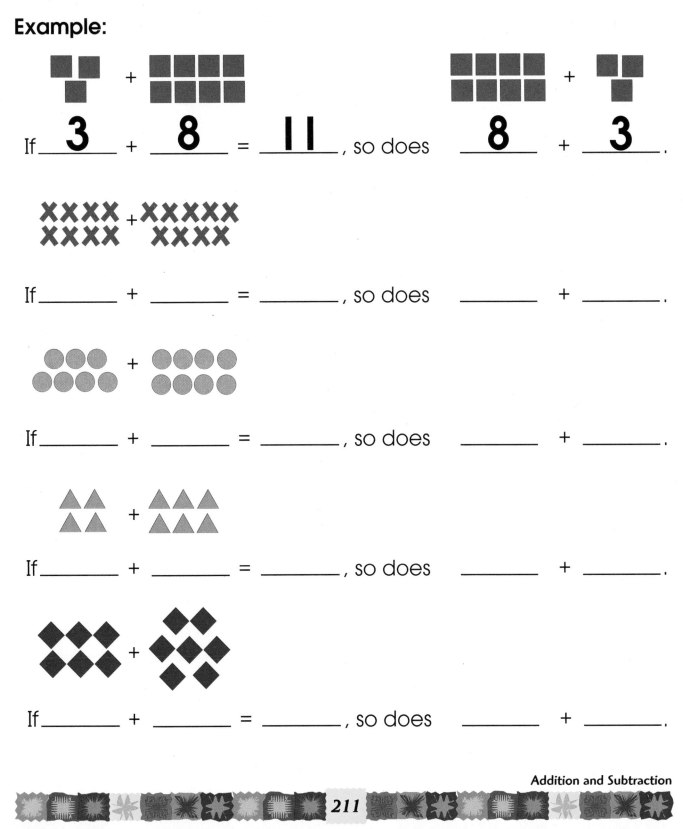

If ___3___ + ___8___ = ___II___ , so does ___8___ + ___3___ .

If _____ + _____ = _____ , so does _____ + _____ .

If _____ + _____ = _____ , so does _____ + _____ .

If _____ + _____ = _____ , so does _____ + _____ .

If _____ + _____ = _____ , so does _____ + _____ .

Addition and Subtraction

Name _____

When adding three numbers, **add** two numbers first, then **add** the third to that sum. To decide which two numbers to add first, try one of these strategies.

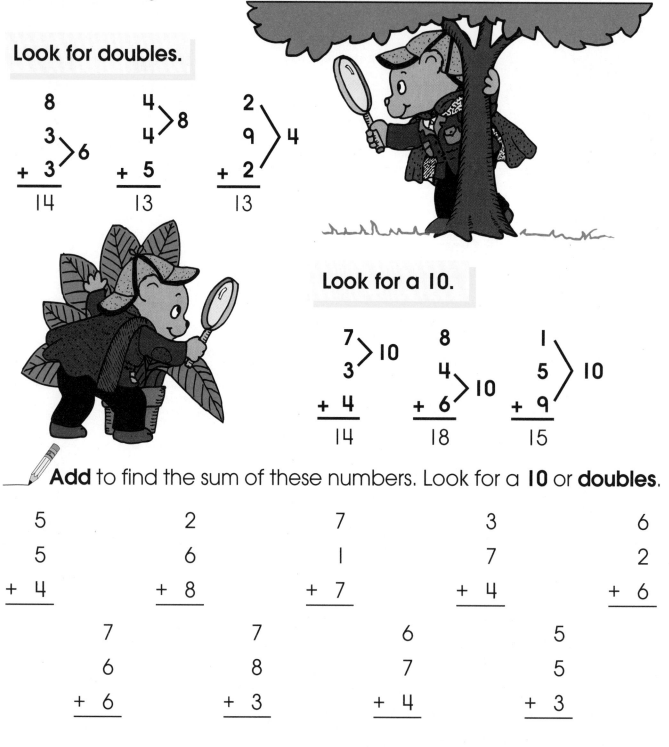

Look for doubles.

```
  8              4              2
  3 }6          4 }8          9 }4
+ 3           + 5           + 2
 14            13            13
```

Look for a 10.

```
  7 }10         8              1
  3            4 }10          5 }10
+ 4           + 6           + 9
 14            18            15
```

Add to find the sum of these numbers. Look for a **10** or **doubles**.

```
   5        2        7        3        6
   5        6        1        7        2
 + 4      + 8      + 7      + 4      + 6


   7        7        6        5
   6        8        7        5
 + 6      + 3      + 4      + 3
```

Addition and Subtraction

212

Name _____

Add to find the sum. If the sum is 11 or more, **color** the cone **brown**. If the sum is less than 11, **color** the cone yellow.

Addition and Subtraction

Name _____

Solve each row from left to right. ✏️ **Write** the letters on the lines below to answer the riddle. **Connect** the dots in the order of the answers.

E	3	**H**	2	**S**	4	**Y**	7	**A**	4	**O**	7
	4		9		4		9		5		7
+	7	+	1	+	7	+	3	+	8	+	2

B	9	**P**	8	**T**	9	**I**	5	**V**	6	**R**	9
	8		4		9		2		2		6
+	5	+	6	+	6	+	1	+	3	+	6

What do a race car and a zebra have in common?

‾22‾ ‾16‾ ‾24‾ ‾12‾   ‾12‾ ‾17‾ ‾11‾ ‾14‾

‾15‾ ‾24‾ ‾21‾ ‾8‾ ‾18‾ ‾14‾ ‾15‾

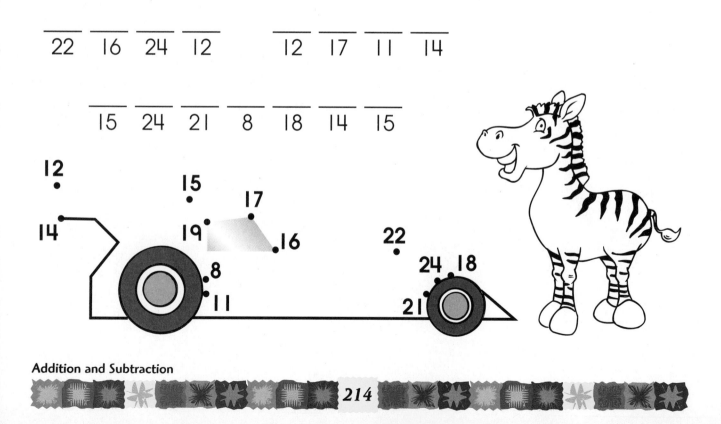

Name _____

Add to find the sums. **Write** the letters on the lines.

What do you call a mummy who eats crackers in bed?

$\overline{}$ $\overline{}$ $\overline{}$ $\overline{}$ $\overline{}$ $\overline{}$ $\overline{}$ $\overline{}$ $\overline{}$ $\overline{}$ $\overline{}$ $\overline{}$
15   14   12   16   9   17   7   11   18   13   8   10

M $7 + 3 + 1 =$	M $7 + 0 + 2 =$	A $6 + 4 + 5 =$
C $5 + 6 + 3 =$	Y $2 + 2 + 6 =$	M $5 + 3 + 5 =$
M $8 + 2 + 7 =$	R $5 + 4 + 3 =$	Y $4 + 2 + 1 =$
U $8 + 3 + 5 =$	M $6 + 2 + 0 =$	U $8 + 1 + 9 =$

Use the number line to **count back**.

Example: **8, _7_ , _6_**

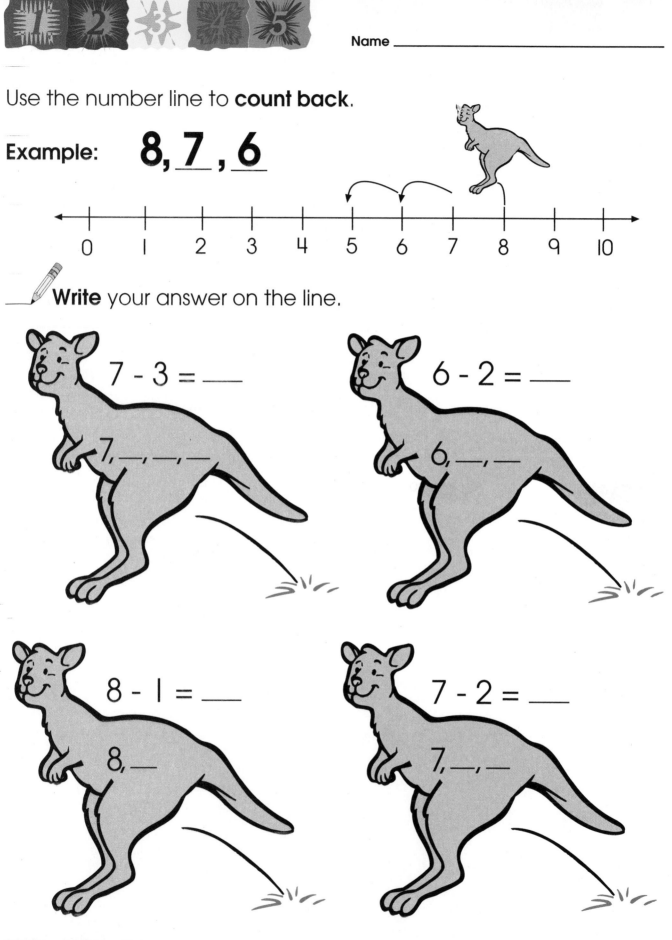

```
←——|———|———|———|———|———|———|———|———|———|———→
    0   I   2   3   4   5   6   7   8   9   10
```

Write your answer on the line.

7 - 3 = ___

7, ___ , ___

6 - 2 = ___

6, ___ , ___

8 - 1 = ___

8, ___

7 - 2 = ___

7, ___ , ___

Name _____

Look at the pictures. Write the answer to each subtraction sentence.

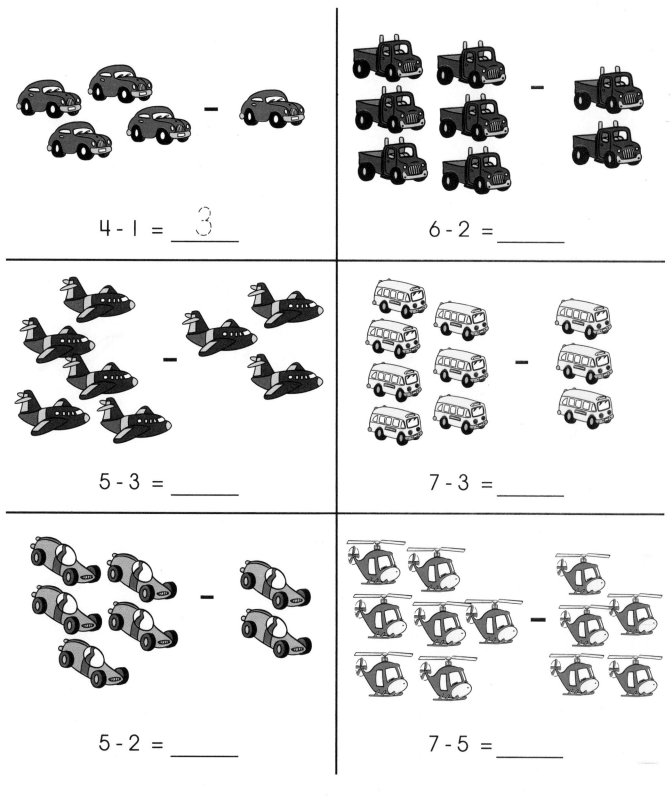

4 - 1 = _3_

6 - 2 = _____

5 - 3 = _____

7 - 3 = _____

5 - 2 = _____

7 - 5 = _____

Addition and Subtraction

Name _____

Look at the pictures. ✏ **Write** the answer to each subtraction sentence.

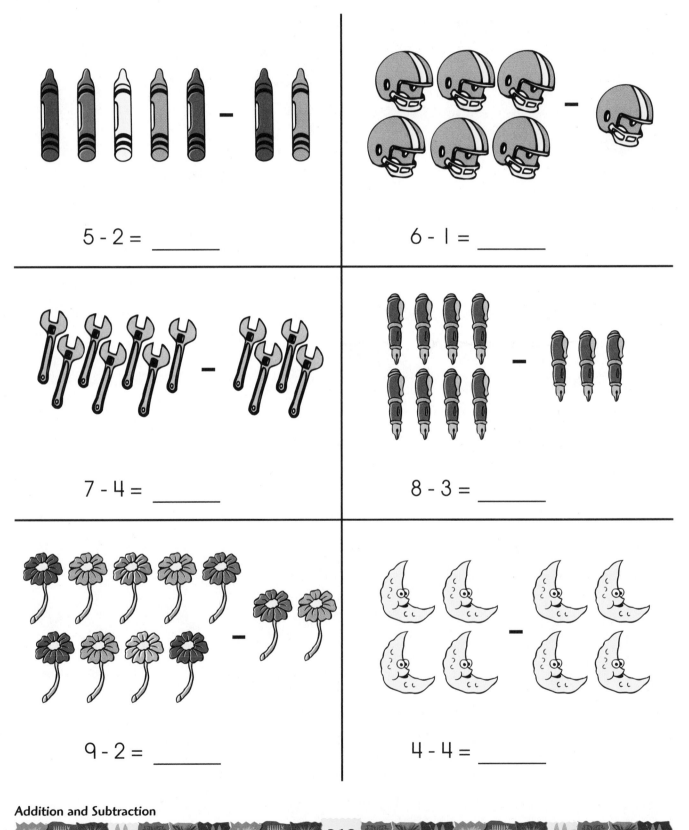

5 - 2 = _____

6 - 1 = _____

7 - 4 = _____

8 - 3 = _____

9 - 2 = _____

4 - 4 = _____

Addition and Subtraction

Name _____

Solve the subtraction sentences below. ✏ **Write** each answer on a rubber duck.

5 - 4

1 - 0

4 - 2

2 - 1

3 - 1

3 - 2

4 - 1

1 - 1

5 - 1

5 - 2

Name _____

Color the two numbers in each box that show the given difference.

Difference of 1

6	4
3	8

3	1
5	6

4	0
1	7

Difference of 1

3	7
1	8

2	3
5	7

6	3
9	7

Difference of 2

3	0
7	1

3	8
6	9

7	1
4	5

Difference of 2

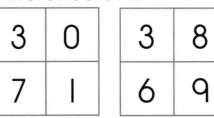

3	4
8	2

7	4
10	5

10	8
5	4

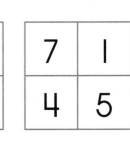

Difference of 0

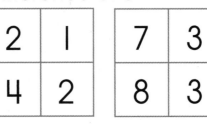

2	1
4	2

7	3
8	3

5	6
5	4

Name _____

✏️ **Circle** the two numbers next to each other that make the given difference. Find as many as you can in each row.

Difference of **1**

2	3	0	8	7	2	9	10	6	5	1	4	4	3

Difference of **1**

8	4	5	3	7	1	2	4	9	8	0	1	7	6

Difference of **2**

5	4	2	3	1	0	2	5	8	9	7	6	8	5

Difference of **2**

7	5	10	8	1	4	6	3	1	6	7	9	2	0

Difference of **3**

1	6	3	2	8	4	7	6	10	7	3	9	5	2

Name _____

✏️ **Draw** an **X** on the nose of each worm with the wrong answer. Find 6 wrong answers.

The worms show:

$17 - 8 = 9$

$7 - 5 = 2$

$10 - 6 = 4$

$5 - 5 = 0$

$13 - 4 = 8$

$8 - 2 = 6$

$11 - 5 = 7$

$11 - 7 = 3$

$14 - 5 = 9$

$9 - 0 = 9$

$12 - 3 = 8$

$15 - 6 = 8$

$15 - 9 = 5$

$10 - 3 = 7$

$14 - 6 = 8$

Addition and Subtraction

Name _____

Solve the subtraction sentences below. Use the code to **color** the picture.

0 — green   2 — blue   4 — black
1 — brown   3 — purple   5 — pink

Name _____

Count the candy in each dish. **Write** the number on the line by each dish. **Circle** each problem with the same answer.

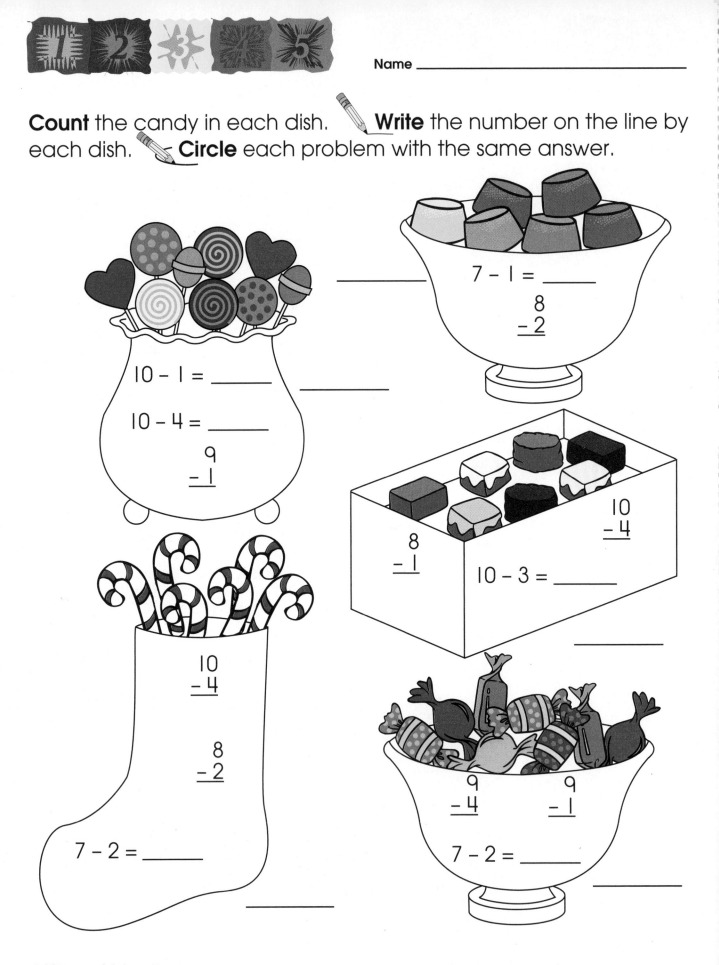

_____

$7 - 1 =$ _____

$\begin{array}{r} 8 \\ -2 \\ \hline \end{array}$

$10 - 1 =$ _____   _____

$10 - 4 =$ _____

$\begin{array}{r} 9 \\ -1 \\ \hline \end{array}$

$\begin{array}{r} 10 \\ -4 \\ \hline \end{array}$

$\begin{array}{r} 8 \\ -1 \\ \hline \end{array}$

$10 - 3 =$ _____

_____

$\begin{array}{r} 10 \\ -4 \\ \hline \end{array}$

$\begin{array}{r} 8 \\ -2 \\ \hline \end{array}$

$7 - 2 =$ _____

$\begin{array}{r} 9 \\ -4 \\ \hline \end{array}$ $\begin{array}{r} 9 \\ -1 \\ \hline \end{array}$

$7 - 2 =$ _____

_____

_____

Name _____

✏️ **Write** the answers to the subtraction problems. Use the code to find the secret message.

Code:

7	5	2	6	4	3
K	T	Y	E	W	A

PLEASE, DON'T EVER

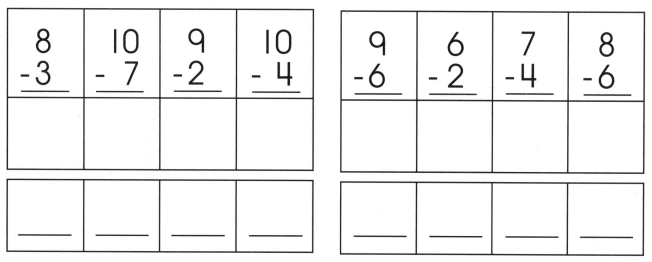

8 -3	10 - 7	9 -2	10 - 4
___	___	___	___

9 -6	6 - 2	7 -4	8 -6
___	___	___	___

MY MATH!

Name _____

Subtract. Write the answer in the space. Then, **color** the spaces according to the answers.

1 — white　　2 — **purple**　　3 — **black**　　4 — green　　5 — yellow
6 — **blue**　　7 — pink　　8 — **gray**　　9 — orange　　10 — red

Name _____

✏ **Subtract** to find the difference.

6	11	15	11
− 3	− 4	− 6	− 6

12	10	12	10	13	8	12
− 3	− 6	− 4	− 5	− 5	− 7	− 3

14	17	11	15	14	10	13
− 8	− 9	− 8	− 7	− 9	− 3	− 4

9	12	14	8	12	18	14
− 6	− 9	− 6	− 5	− 7	− 9	− 6

8	12	18	14	13	13	17
− 5	− 7	− 9	− 6	− 8	− 6	− 8

Name _____

Look at the pictures. ✏ **Write** **+** or **–** in the circles. **Write** the answers to the number sentences.

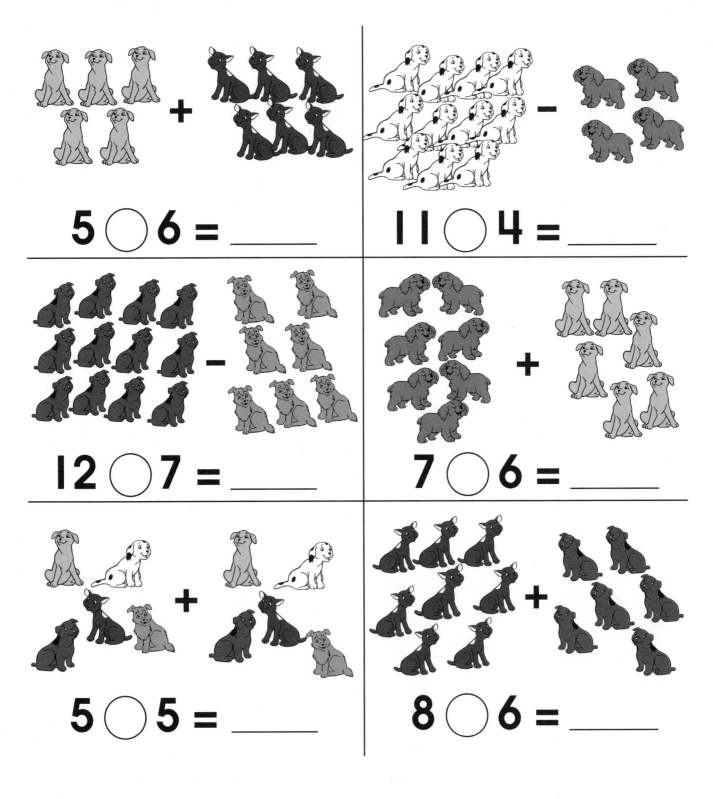

5 ◯ 6 = _____

11 ◯ 4 = _____

12 ◯ 7 = _____

7 ◯ 6 = _____

5 ◯ 5 = _____

8 ◯ 6 = _____

Name _____

Write **+** or **–** in the magnifying glass to make each problem correct. **Circle** the four problems that will not work with either sign.

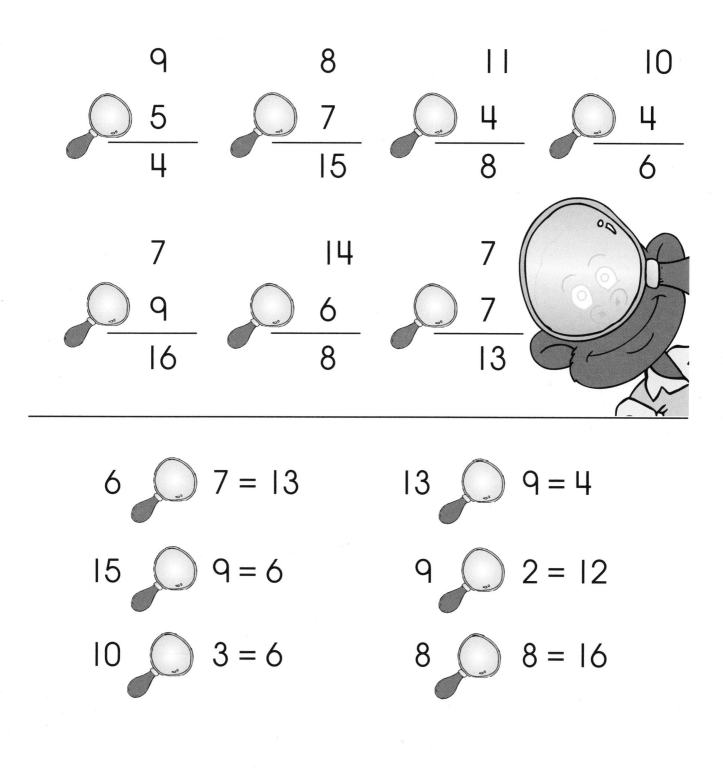

9	8	11	10
5	7	4	4
4	15	8	6

7	14	7
9	6	7
16	8	13

6 ⊙ 7 = 13   13 ⊙ 9 = 4

15 ⊙ 9 = 6   9 ⊙ 2 = 12

10 ⊙ 3 = 6   8 ⊙ 8 = 16

Name _____

Should you add or subtract? The key words "in all" tell you to add. The key word "left" tells you to subtract. Circle the key words and write **+** or **–** in the circles. Then, solve the problems. The first one is done for you.

1. The pet store has 3 large dogs and 5 small dogs. How many dogs are there in all?

$$3 \bigoplus 5 = \underline{\textbf{8}}$$

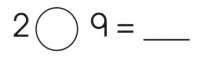

2. The pet store had 9 parrots and then sold 4 of them. How many parrots does the pet store have left?

$$9 \bigcirc 4 = \underline{}$$

4. The pet store gave Linda's class 2 adult gerbils and 9 young ones. How many gerbils did Linda's class get in all?

$$2 \bigcirc 9 = \underline{}$$

3. At the pet store, 3 of the 8 kittens were sold. How many kittens are left in the pet store?

$$8 \bigcirc 3 = \underline{}$$

5. The monkey at the pet store has 5 rubber toys and 4 wooden toys. How many toys does the monkey have in all?

$$5 \bigcirc 4 = \underline{}$$

Addition and Subtraction

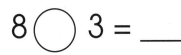

Name _____

Write the answer to the number problem under each picture.
Write + or **–** to show if you should add or subtract.

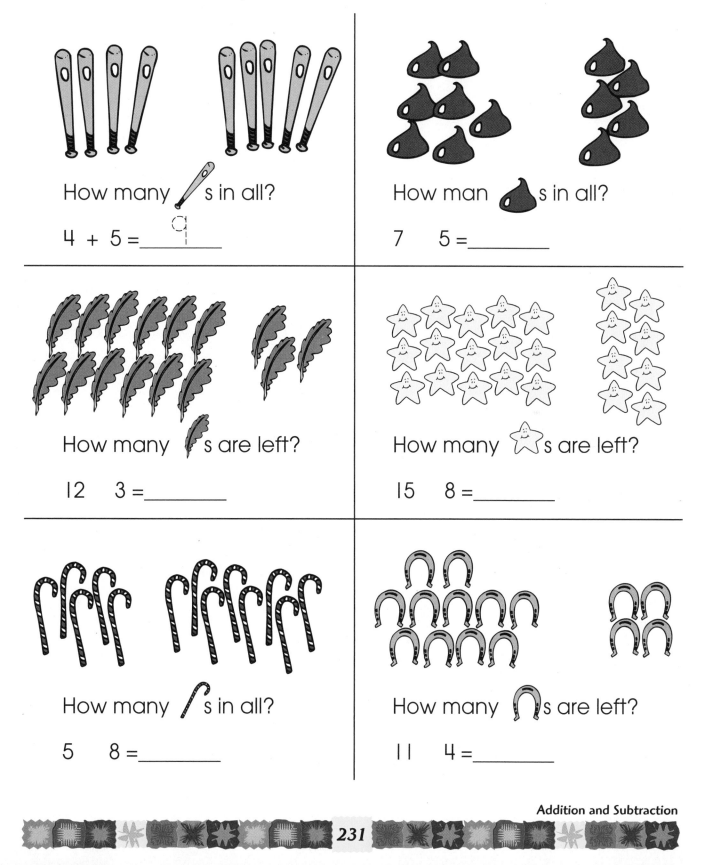

How many 🏏s in all?

4 + 5 = _____9_____

How man 🍫s in all?

7 ___ 5 = _____

How many 🍃s are left?

12 ___ 3 = _____

How many ⭐s are left?

15 ___ 8 = _____

How many 🍬s in all?

5 ___ 8 = _____

How many ⊓s are left?

11 ___ 4 = _____

Name _____

Write the answer to the number problem under each picture.
Write **+** or **–** to show if you should add or subtract.

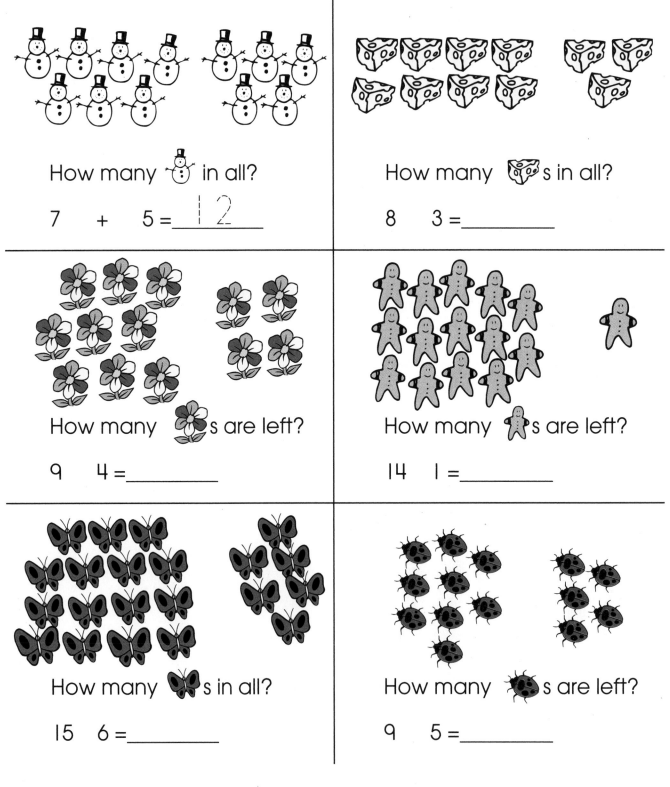

How many ☃ in all?

7   +   5 = __12__

How many 🧀 s in all?

8   3 = _____

How many 🌸 s are left?

9   4 = _____

How many 🍪 s are left?

14   1 = _____

How many 🦋 s in all?

15   6 = _____

How many 🐞 s are left?

9   5 = _____

Addition and Subtraction

Name _____

Draw a line under the question that matches the picture. Then, solve the problems.

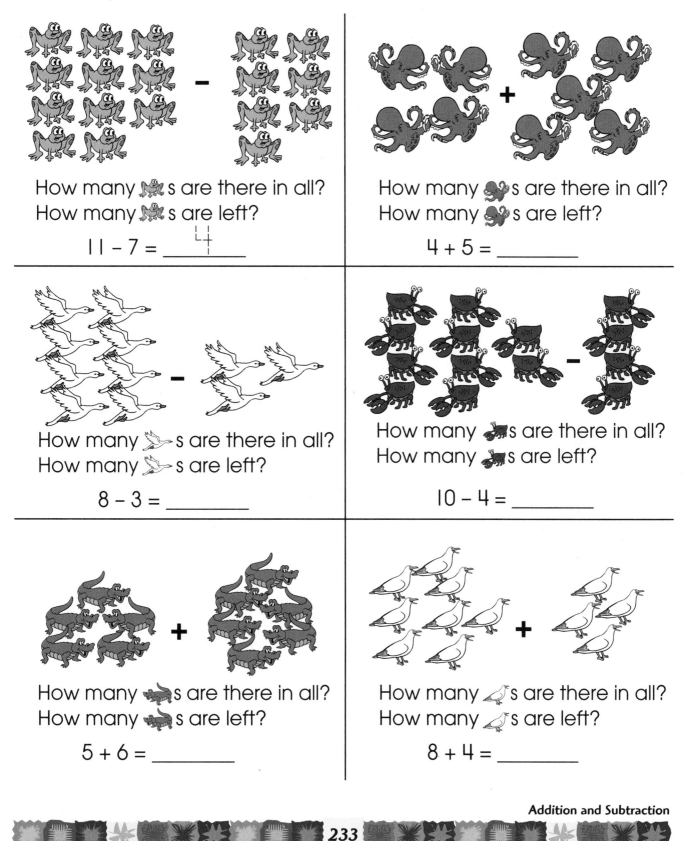

How many 🐸s are there in all?
How many 🐸s are left?

$11 - 7 =$ ___4___

How many 🐙s are there in all?
How many 🐙s are left?

$4 + 5 =$ ___

How many 🦢s are there in all?
How many 🦢s are left?

$8 - 3 =$ ___

How many 🦀s are there in all?
How many 🦀s are left?

$10 - 4 =$ ___

How many 🐊s are there in all?
How many 🐊s are left?

$5 + 6 =$ ___

How many 🕊s are there in all?
How many 🕊s are left?

$8 + 4 =$ ___

Name _____

Add or **subtract** to solve each problem. **Circle** the answers that are less than 10.

Example:

$$3 \atop +1 \over \textcircled{4}$$

$$3 \atop -1 \over \textcircled{2}$$

$$\begin{array}{r} 9 \\ +3 \\ \hline \end{array}$$
$$\begin{array}{r} 6 \\ -2 \\ \hline \end{array}$$
$$\begin{array}{r} 12 \\ -1 \\ \hline \end{array}$$
$$\begin{array}{r} 18 \\ +1 \\ \hline \end{array}$$
$$\begin{array}{r} 15 \\ -6 \\ \hline \end{array}$$

$$\begin{array}{r} 7 \\ +6 \\ \hline \end{array}$$
$$\begin{array}{r} 16 \\ -9 \\ \hline \end{array}$$
$$\begin{array}{r} 10 \\ -3 \\ \hline \end{array}$$
$$\begin{array}{r} 14 \\ +5 \\ \hline \end{array}$$
$$\begin{array}{r} 16 \\ -8 \\ \hline \end{array}$$

$$\begin{array}{r} 8 \\ +7 \\ \hline \end{array}$$
$$\begin{array}{r} 12 \\ +2 \\ \hline \end{array}$$
$$\begin{array}{r} 13 \\ -4 \\ \hline \end{array}$$
$$\begin{array}{r} 17 \\ +2 \\ \hline \end{array}$$
$$\begin{array}{r} 9 \\ +9 \\ \hline \end{array}$$

Addition and Subtraction

Name _____

Add or **subtract** to solve each problem. Use the code to **color** the fruit.

3 — yellow   5 — orange   7 — yellow   9 — red
4 — red   6 — purple   8 — green   10 — brown

9
- 4

3
+ 7
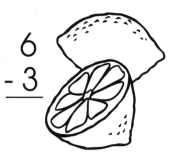

6
- 3

1
+ 3
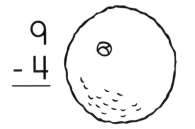

9
- 2

7
+ 2

9
- 1
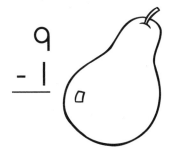

6
+ 3
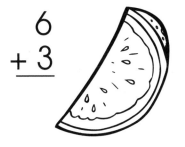

8
- 2
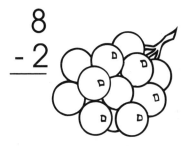

Addition and Subtraction

235

Name _____

Write the answers to the addition and subtraction problems below.

10	7	4	6	4
− 6	+ 3	− 2	− 2	+ 1

6	5	7	6
+ 4	+ 4	− 1	− 3

4	1	2	8	2	10	9
+ 3	+ 9	− 1	− 6	+ 1	− 3	− 4

3	2	6	5	5	8	5
+ 5	+ 8	− 3	+ 5	− 3	+ 2	− 4

10	5	5	9	2	3	8
− 8	− 1	+ 2	+ 2	+ 6	+ 7	+ 1

Two-Digit Addition and Subtraction

Look at the examples. Follow the steps to **add**.

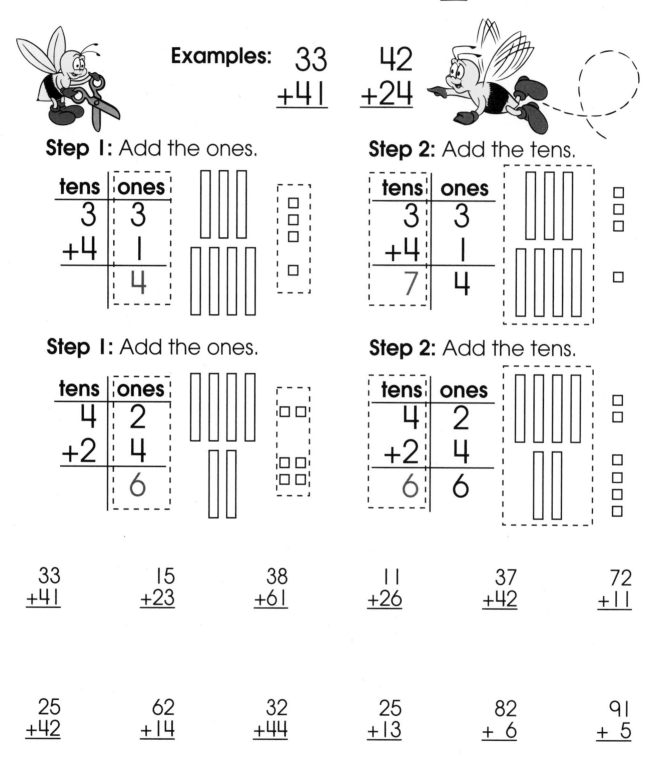

Examples: 33   42
            +41 +24

Step 1: Add the ones.

tens	ones
3	3
+4	1
	4

Step 2: Add the tens.

tens	ones
3	3
+4	1
7	4

Step 1: Add the ones.

tens	ones
4	2
+2	4
	6

Step 2: Add the tens.

tens	ones
4	2
+2	4
6	6

33	15	38	11	37	72
+41	+23	+61	+26	+42	+11

25	62	32	25	82	91
+42	+14	+44	+13	+ 6	+ 5

Name _____

Add the ones, then the tens in each problem. Then, **write** the sum in the blank.

Example:

  2 tens and 6 ones
+ 1 ten   and 3 ones
_____

  3 tens and 9 ones = 39

  1 ten   and 4 ones
+ 3 tens and 3 ones
_____

___ tens and ___ ones = ___

  2 tens and 5 ones
+ 2 tens and 3 ones
_____

___ tens and ___ ones = ___

  1 ten   and 6 ones
+ 5 tens and 1 one
_____

___ tens and ___ ones = ___

  1 ten   and 3 ones
+ 1 ten   and 1 one
_____

___ tens and ___ ones = ___

  2 tens and 5 ones
+ 2 tens and 0 ones
_____

___ tens and ___ ones = ___

  1 ten   and 5 ones
+ 2 tens and 4 ones
_____

___ tens and ___ ones = ___

  7 tens and 6 ones
+ 2 tens and 2 ones
_____

___ tens and ___ ones = ___

Two-Digit Addition and Subtraction

Add to solve the problems. **Add** the ones first. Then, **add** the tens.

tens	ones
2	5
+1	4

tens	ones
5	3
+3	2

tens	ones
7	1
+2	8

tens	ones
4	4
+3	2

tens	ones
5	1
+3	7

tens	ones
2	6
+5	2

tens	ones
2	6
+4	2

tens	ones
3	7
+5	1

tens	ones
1	9
+3	0

Two-Digit Addition and Subtraction

Name _____

Add the total points scored in each game. Remember to **add** the ones first, then the tens.

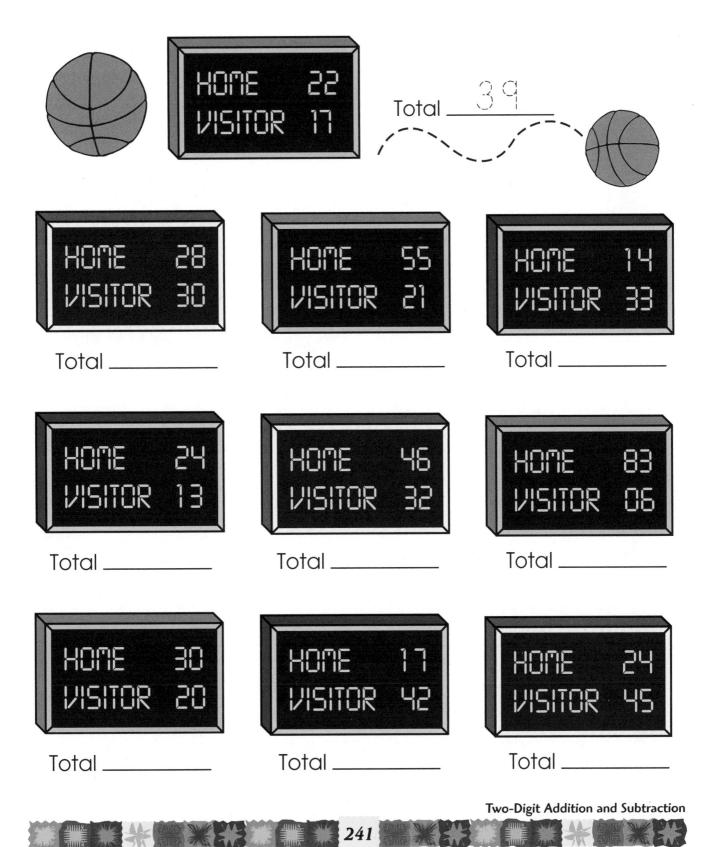

HOME   22
VISITOR 17

Total ___39___

HOME   28
VISITOR 30

Total _____

HOME   55
VISITOR 21

Total _____

HOME   14
VISITOR 33

Total _____

HOME   24
VISITOR 13

Total _____

HOME   46
VISITOR 32

Total _____

HOME   83
VISITOR 06

Total _____

HOME   30
VISITOR 20

Total _____

HOME   17
VISITOR 42

Total _____

HOME   24
VISITOR 45

Total _____

Two-Digit Addition and Subtraction

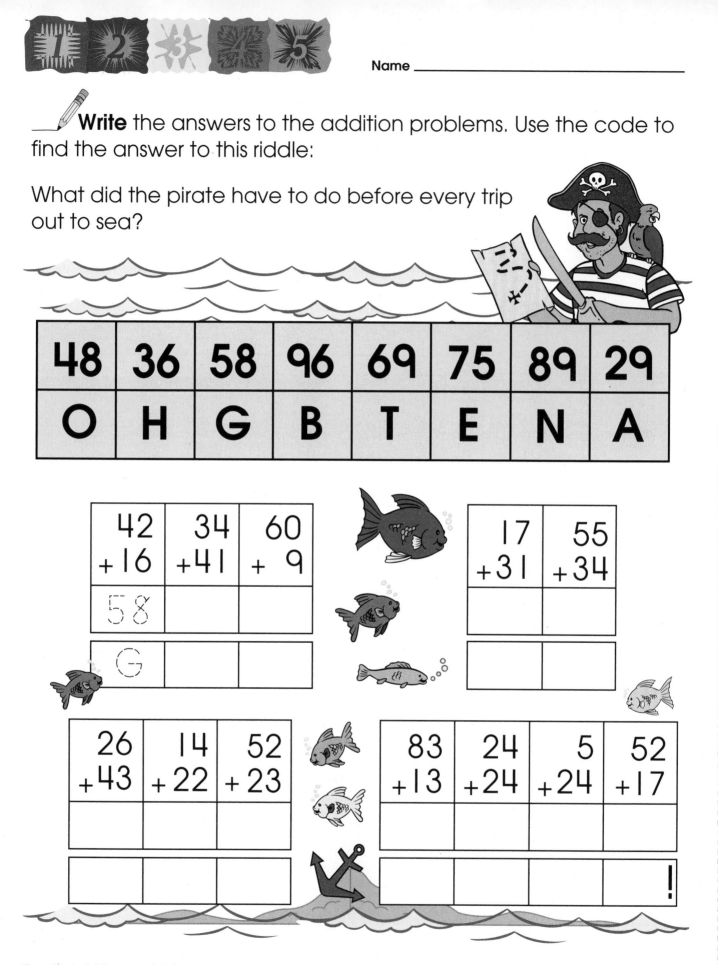

Name _____

Write the answers to the addition problems. Use the code to find the answer to this riddle:

What did the pirate have to do before every trip out to sea?

48	36	58	96	69	75	89	29
O	H	G	B	T	E	N	A

42	34	60
+16	+41	+ 9
58		

G		

17	55
+31	+34

26	14	52
+43	+22	+23

83	24	5	52
+13	+24	+24	+17

			!

Two-Digit Addition and Subtraction

Name _____

Write the answers to each problem to find the number of bees in each hive. Use the letters to solve the riddle.

K
26
+13
____

M
82
+15
____

L
12
+32
____

E
34
+45
____

J
92
+ 6
____

R
46
+31
____

B
61
+22
____

A
56
+12
____

C
70
+15
____

The honey was too hard to get so Ted E. Bear ate something else. What was it?

—— —— —— —— ——
83   44   68   85   39

"—— —— —— —— ——   —— —— ——"
 83   79   68   77   79   98   68   97

Look at the example. Follow the steps to **subtract**.

Examples:

28
-14

24
-12

Step 1: Subtract the ones.

tens	ones
2	8
-1	4
	4

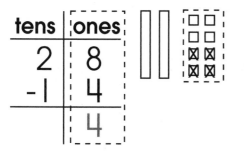

Step 2: Subtract the tens.

tens	ones
2	8
-1	4
1	4

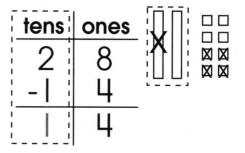

Step 1: Subtract the ones.

tens	ones
2	4
-1	2
	2

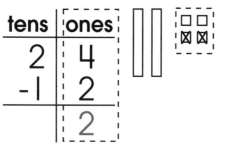

Step 2: Subtract the tens.

tens	ones
2	4
-1	2
1	2

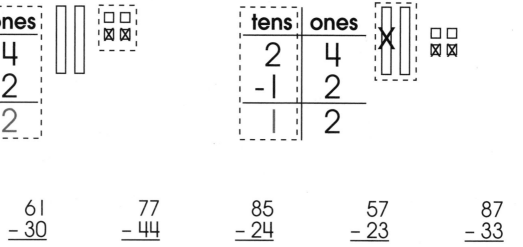

24	61	77	85	57	87
-12	-30	-44	-24	-23	-33

Two-Digit Addition and Subtraction

Name _____

Count the tens and ones and **write** the numbers. Then, **subtract** to solve the problems. ✏️

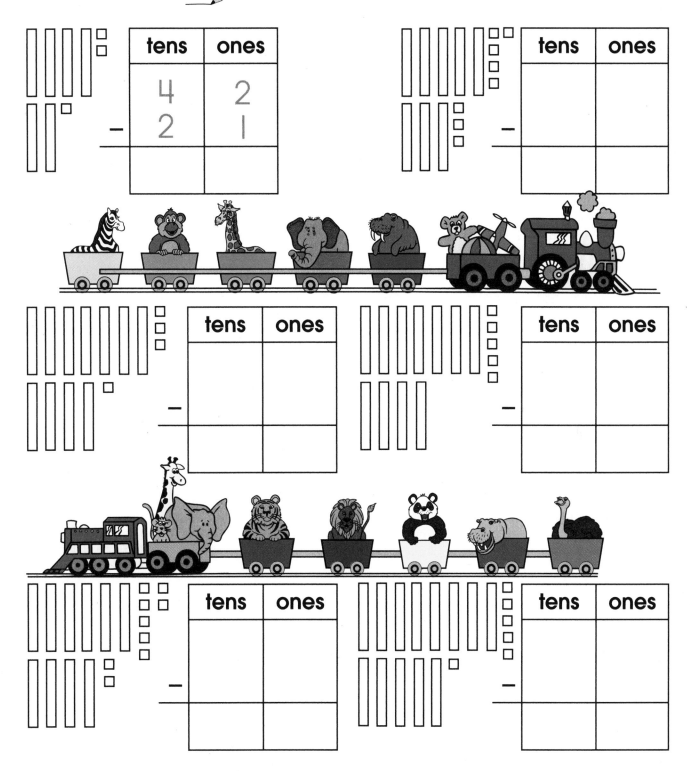

tens	ones
4	2
2	1

tens	ones

tens	ones

tens	ones

tens	ones

tens	ones

Two-Digit Addition and Subtraction

Name _____

Subtract to solve the problems. **Circle** the answers. **Color** the cookies with answers greater than 30.

49
− 23

16 (26) 25

67
− 41

26 15 62

58
− 37

81 11 21

75
− 50

20 25 35

86
− 21

67 86 65

64
− 52

12 26 16

97
− 65

31 33 32

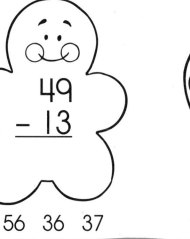

49
− 13

56 36 37

77
− 43

34 43 39

Two-Digit Addition and Subtraction

Write the answers to the subtraction problems.

u
95
− 14

n
68
− 47

t
80
− 20

r
79
− 38

a
83
− 52

h
84
− 23

y
75
− 31

i
99
− 29

c
98
− 36

o
84
− 30

e
98
− 16

g
74
− 42

s
58
− 38

p
82
− 40

Use the answers and the letters on the baseballs to **solve** the code.

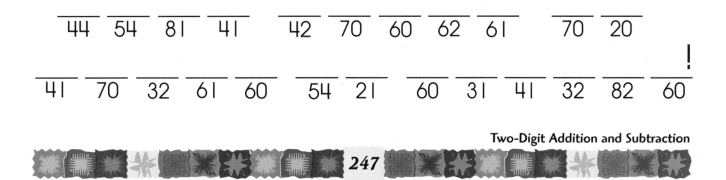

44 54 81 41   42 70 60 62 61   70 20

41 70 32 61 60   54 21   60 31 41 32 82 60 !

Two-Digit Addition and Subtraction

Name _____

The players warm up before each game. **Subtract** to find out how many of each exercise the coach wants the players to do.

$$\begin{array}{r} 38 \\ -\ 13 \\ \hline \end{array}$$
sit-ups

$$\begin{array}{r} 50 \\ -\ 20 \\ \hline \end{array}$$
jumping jacks

$$\begin{array}{r} 17 \\ -\ 7 \\ \hline \end{array}$$
sprints

$$\begin{array}{r} 69 \\ -\ 33 \\ \hline \end{array}$$
toe touches

$$\begin{array}{r} 89 \\ -\ 74 \\ \hline \end{array}$$
crunches

$$\begin{array}{r} 92 \\ -\ 20 \\ \hline \end{array}$$
push-ups

What is your favorite exercise?_____

How many of them can you do?_____

Two-Digit Addition and Subtraction

Name _____

Leon the Lion was very hungry.
Write the answers to the problems to find out how many bones he ate. **Circle** all the differences which are smaller than 20.

$$\begin{array}{r} 56 \\ -42 \\ \hline \end{array} \qquad \begin{array}{r} 39 \\ -18 \\ \hline \end{array} \qquad \begin{array}{r} 44 \\ -21 \\ \hline \end{array} \qquad \begin{array}{r} 26 \\ -13 \\ \hline \end{array} \qquad \begin{array}{r} 67 \\ -35 \\ \hline \end{array}$$

$$\begin{array}{r} 88 \\ -15 \\ \hline \end{array} \qquad \begin{array}{r} 79 \\ -58 \\ \hline \end{array} \qquad \begin{array}{r} 59 \\ -28 \\ \hline \end{array} \qquad \begin{array}{r} 68 \\ -47 \\ \hline \end{array} \qquad \begin{array}{r} 94 \\ -83 \\ \hline \end{array}$$

$$\begin{array}{r} 32 \\ -21 \\ \hline \end{array} \qquad \begin{array}{r} 56 \\ -15 \\ \hline \end{array} \qquad \begin{array}{r} 86 \\ -23 \\ \hline \end{array} \qquad \begin{array}{r} 74 \\ -31 \\ \hline \end{array} \qquad \begin{array}{r} 66 \\ -52 \\ \hline \end{array}$$

Two-Digit Addition and Subtraction

Graphing

Name _____

Count the apples in each row. **Color** the boxes to show how many apples have bites taken out of them.

Example:

1	2	3	4	5	6	7	8

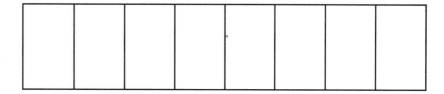

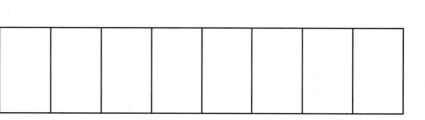

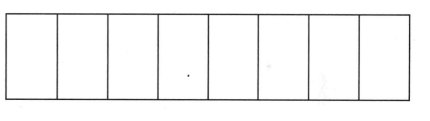

Graphing

Name _____

Make a graph of the animals in the jungle. **Color** one space for each animal.

Name _____

How many of each color flower are there?  **Color** the spaces on the graph below.

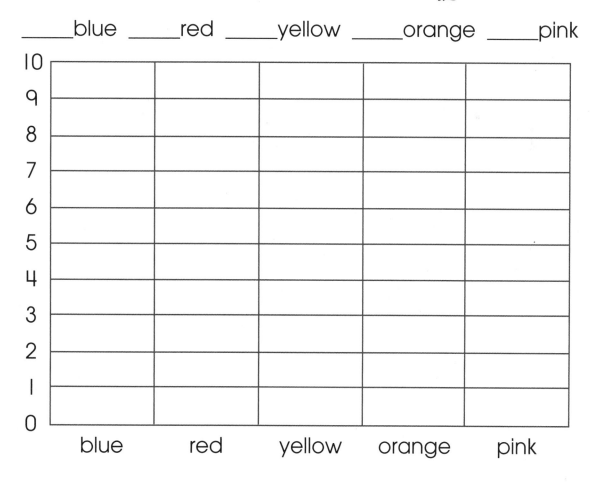

____blue ____red ____yellow ____orange ____pink

10					
9					
8					
7					
6					
5					
4					
3					
2					
1					
0	blue	red	yellow	orange	pink

Name _____

Use the information on the bar graph to **write** the answers to the questions.

Favorite Fruits

	1	2	3	4	5	6	7	8	9	10
Apples										
Oranges										
Bananas										
Pears										
Grapes										

Number of People

1. Which was the favorite fruit? _____

2. Which was the least favorite fruit? _____

3. How many more people picked bananas than pears? _____

4. How many fewer people chose pears than grapes? _____

5. Which fruit was chosen by 6 people? _____

Name _____

The pictures show the weather for one month. **Count** the number of sunny, cloudy, and rainy days.

| |||| |||| |||| | |||| |||| | |||| |

Then make a graph with pictures using the tallies above. This kind of graph is called a **pictograph**.

Weather for 1 month

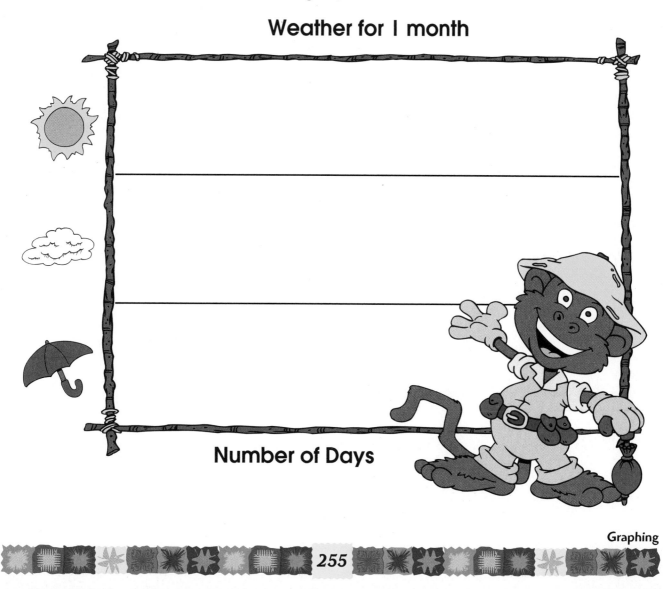

Number of Days

Time

Name _____

A clock can tell you what time it is. A clock has different parts. Read and **trace** each part of the clock.

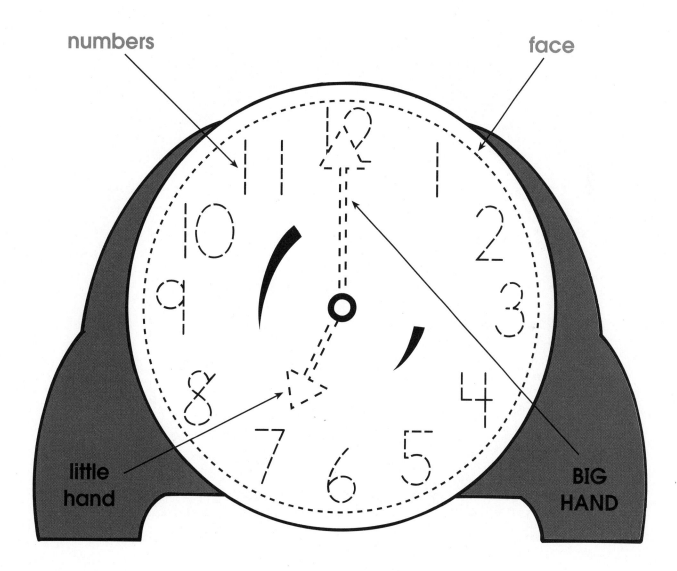

The **BIG HAND** is on **12**.
The **little hand** tells the hour.

Learning to tell time is fun! A clock tells us the time.

Write the numbers on the clock face. **Draw** the **BIG HAND** to **12**. **Draw** the **little hand** to **5**.

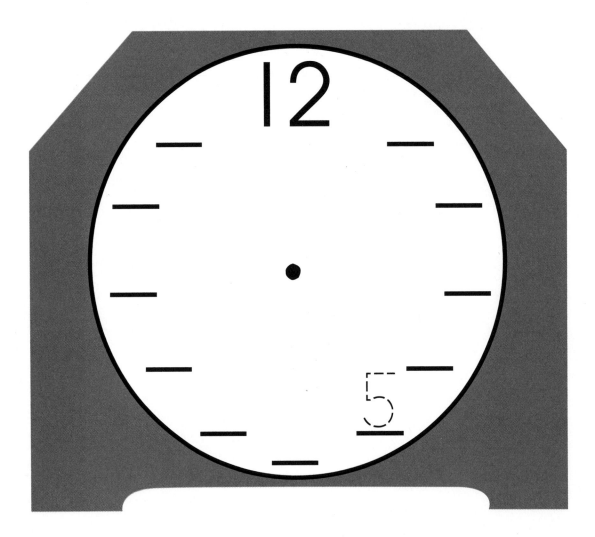

What time is it? _____ o'clock

Name _____

An **hour** is **sixty minutes** long. It takes an **hour** for the **BIG HAND** to go around the clock. When the **BIG HAND** is on **12**, and the **little hand** points to a number, that is the **hour!** The **BIG HAND** is on the **12**. **Color** it **red**. The **little hand** is on the **8**. **Color** it **blue**.

The **BIG HAND** is on _____.
The **little hand** is on_____.

It is _____ o'clock.

Time

259

Name _____

Draw the **little hour hand** on each clock.

4 o'clock

11 o'clock

5 o'clock

Name _____

Circle the **little hour hand** on each clock. What time is it?
Write the time below.

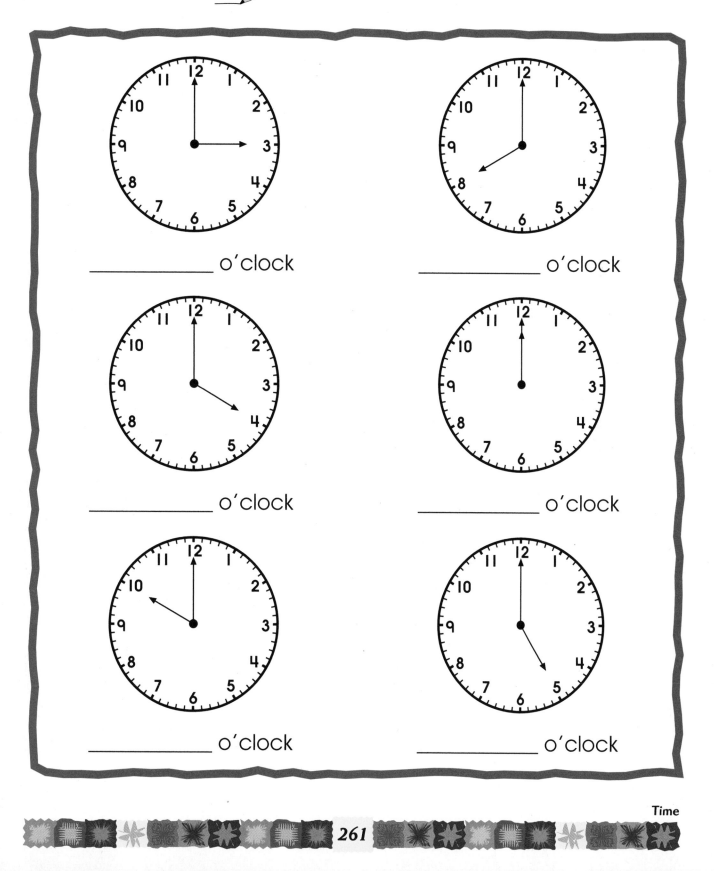

_____ o'clock   _____ o'clock

_____ o'clock   _____ o'clock

_____ o'clock   _____ o'clock

Time

Name _____

Here's the scoop! ✏️ **Draw** the **little hour hand** on each clock.

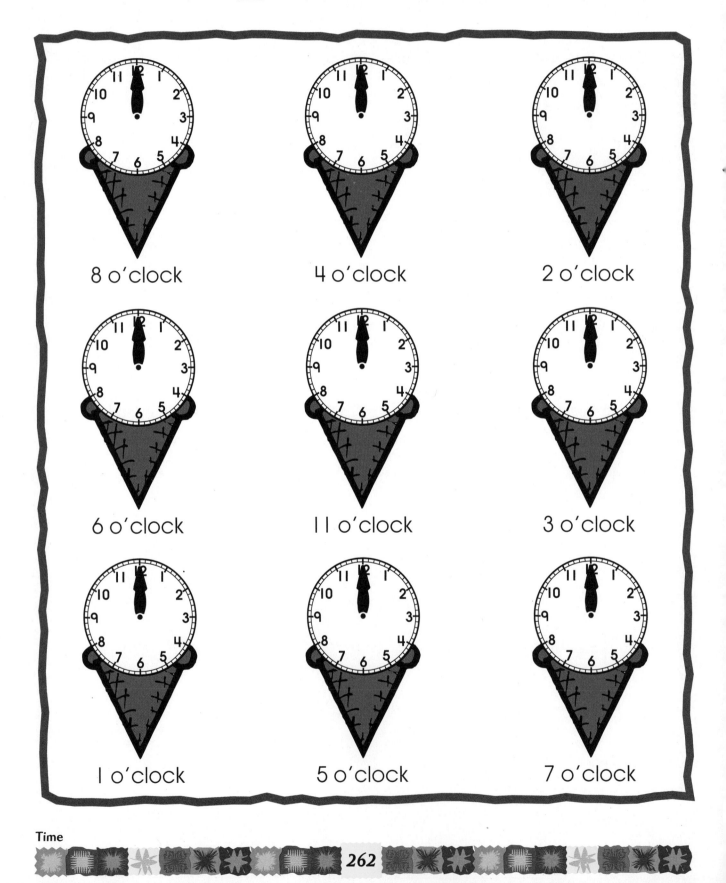

8 o'clock   4 o'clock   2 o'clock

6 o'clock   11 o'clock   3 o'clock

1 o'clock   5 o'clock   7 o'clock

What time is it? ✏ **Write** the time on each clock in the blanks below.

_____ o'clock   _____ o'clock   _____ o'clock

_____ o'clock   _____ o'clock   _____ o'clock

_____ o'clock   _____ o'clock   _____ o'clock

_____ o'clock   _____ o'clock

Time

263

This is how to tell time to the half-hour. This clock face shows the time gone by since 8 o'clock. **Thirty minutes** or **half an hour** has gone by. There are 3 ways to say time to the half-hour. We say **seven-thirty, thirty past seven** or **half-past seven**.

✏ **Write** the time on the clock and the time a half an hour later.

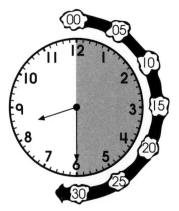

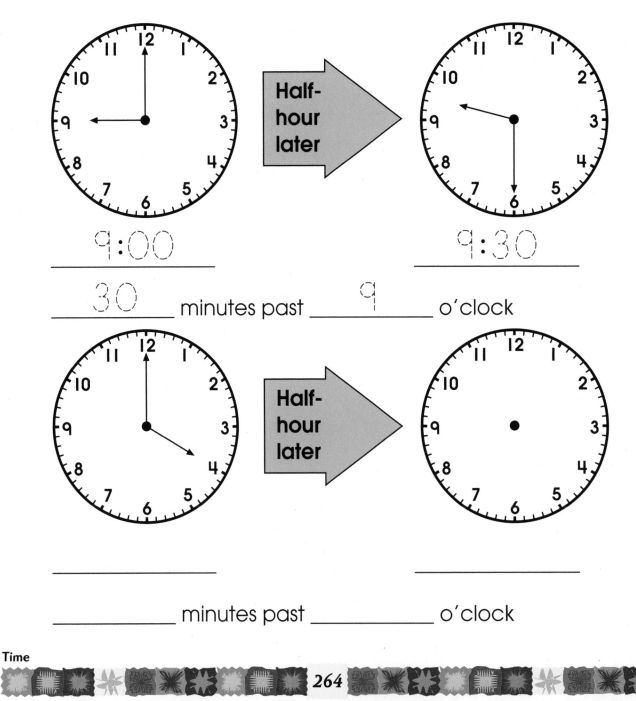

9:00

9:30

____30____ minutes past ____9____ o'clock

_____   _____

_____ minutes past _____ o'clock

Name _____

Write the time on the half-hour.

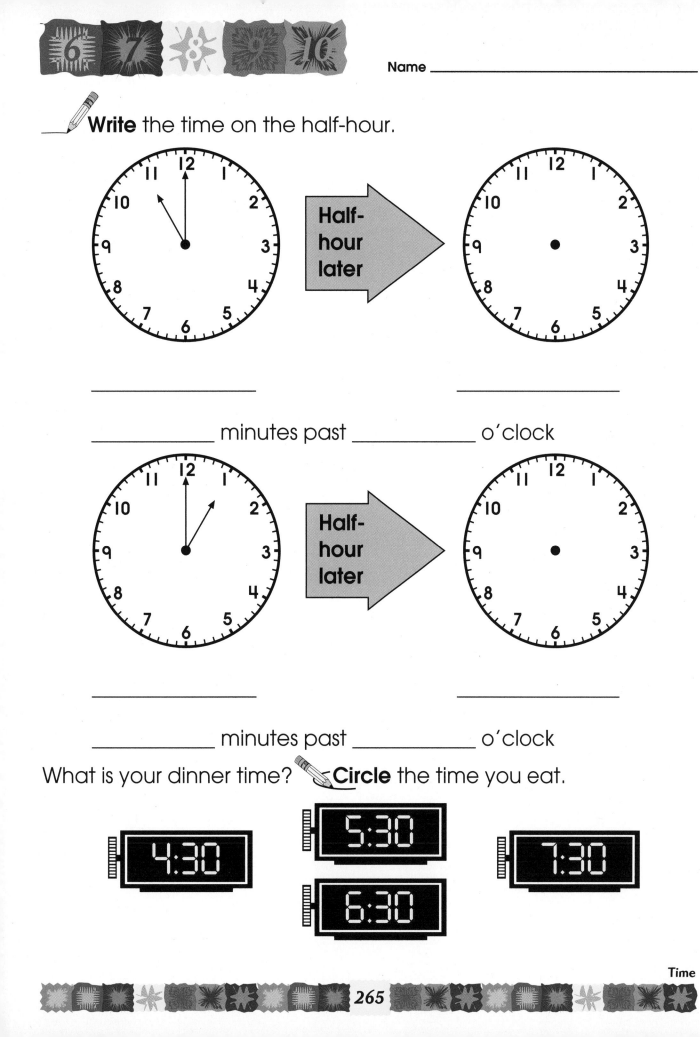

Half-hour later

_____   _____

_____ minutes past _____ o'clock

Half-hour later

_____   _____

_____ minutes past _____ o'clock

What is your dinner time? **Circle** the time you eat.

4:30   5:30   7:30

6:30

Name _____

What time is it? ✎ **Write** the time on each clock in the blanks below.

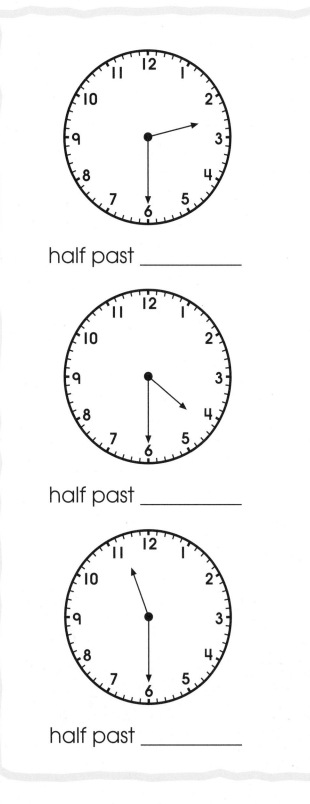

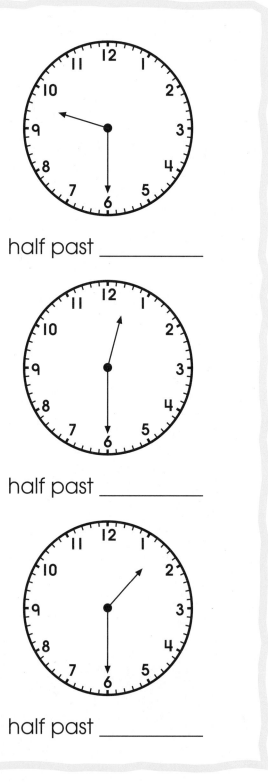

half past _____

half past _____

half past _____

half past _____

half past _____

half past _____

Name _____

Trace the **BIG MINUTE HAND** green. Trace the **little hour hand** red. **Write** the time on the line.

_____   _____

_____   _____

Time

Name _____

Who "nose" these times?

Write the time under each clock. Color the noses.

Name _____

These digital numbers got lost. **Write** them on the right clocks on this page and the next page.

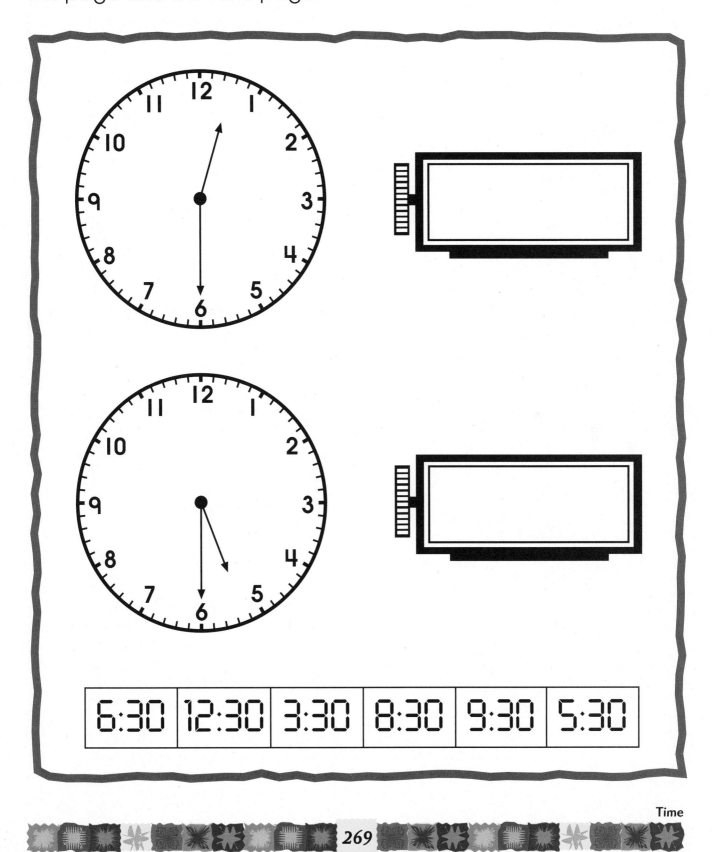

| 6:30 | 12:30 | 3:30 | 8:30 | 9:30 | 5:30 |

Time

Name _____

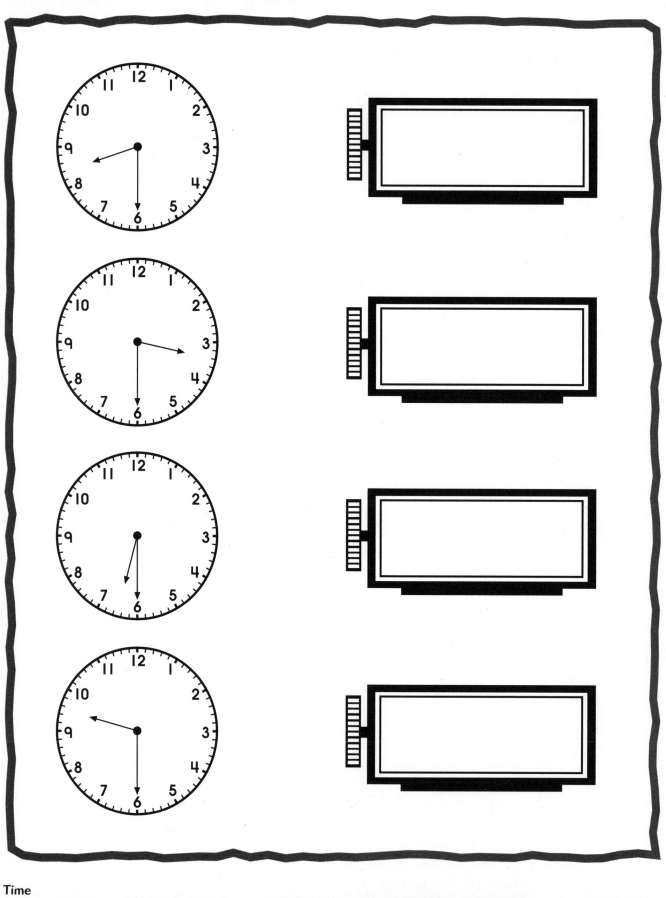

Time

This is how to tell time to the **quarter-hour**. Each **hour** has **60** minutes. An **hour** has **4** **quarter-hours**. A **quarter-hour** is **15 minutes**. This clock face shows a quarter of an hour.
Trace the numbers below.

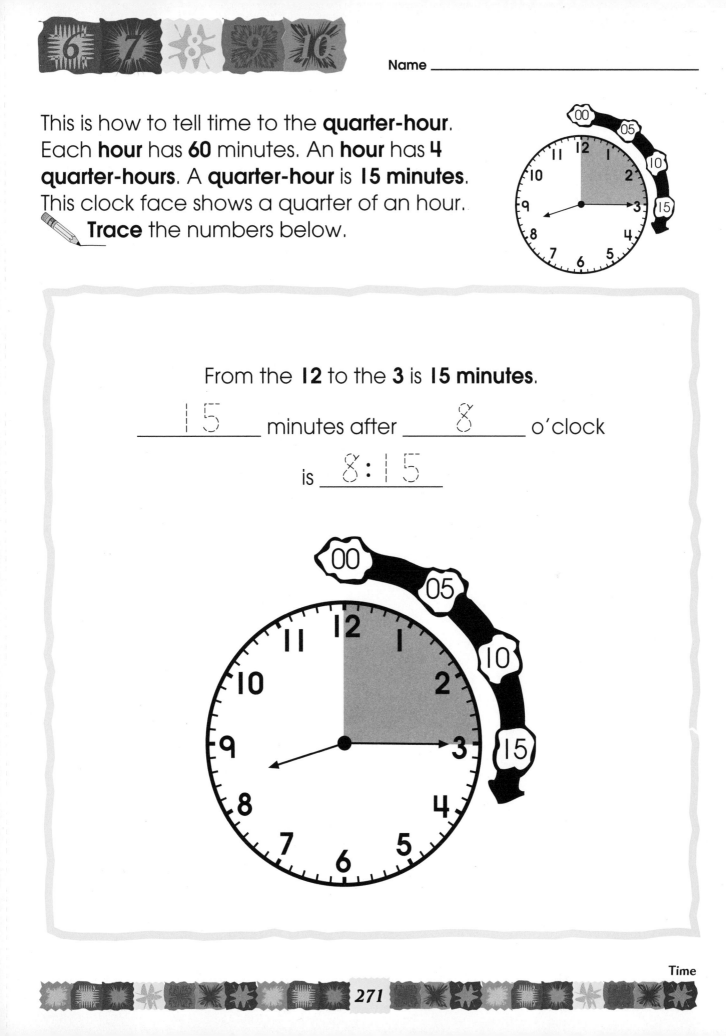

From the **12** to the **3** is **15 minutes**.

_____15_____ minutes after _____8_____ o'clock

is _____8:15_____

Name _____

Each **hour** has **4 quarter-hours**. A **quarter-hour** is **15 minutes**.
Write the times.

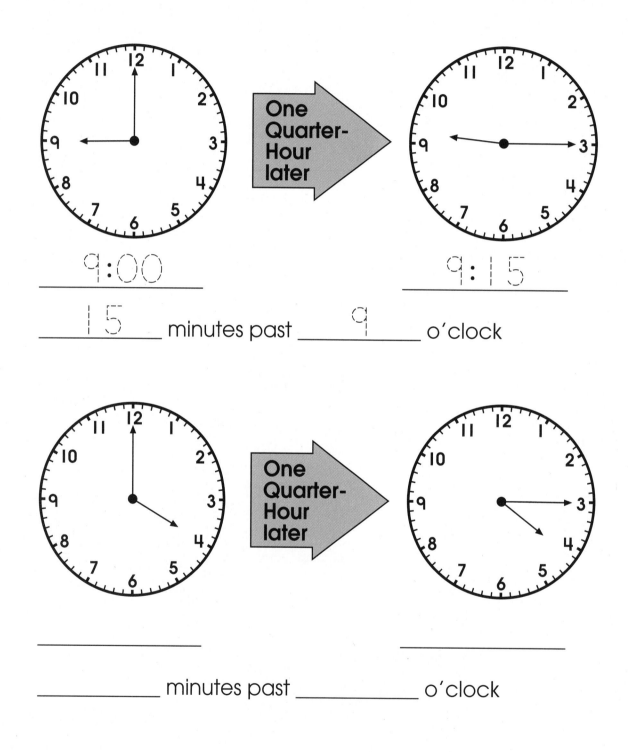

9:00   → One Quarter-Hour later →   9:15

_____15_____ minutes past _____9_____ o'clock

_____   One Quarter-Hour later   _____

_____ minutes past _____ o'clock

Name _____

✏️ **Draw** the hands. **Write** the times.

5:15

_____15_____ minutes after

_____5_____ o'clock

10:15

_____ minutes after

_____ o'clock

2:15

_____ minutes after

_____ o'clock

9:15

_____ minutes after

_____ o'clock

Time

Name _____

Your digital clock has **quarter-hours**, too! It also shows **15 minutes**.
Write the time on each digital clock.

Name _____

✏️ **Circle** the correct digital time.

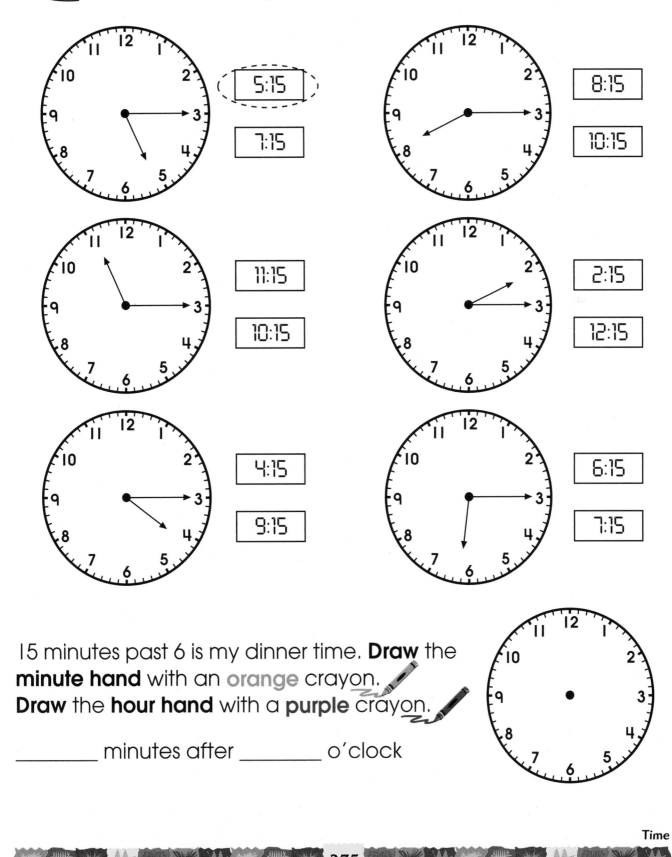

5:15

7:15

8:15

10:15

11:15

10:15

2:15

12:15

4:15

9:15

6:15

7:15

15 minutes past 6 is my dinner time. **Draw** the **minute hand** with an orange crayon. **Draw** the **hour hand** with a **purple** crayon.

_____ minutes after _____ o'clock

Name _____

Count the numbers by 5's to see how many minutes have passed.
Trace the numbers.

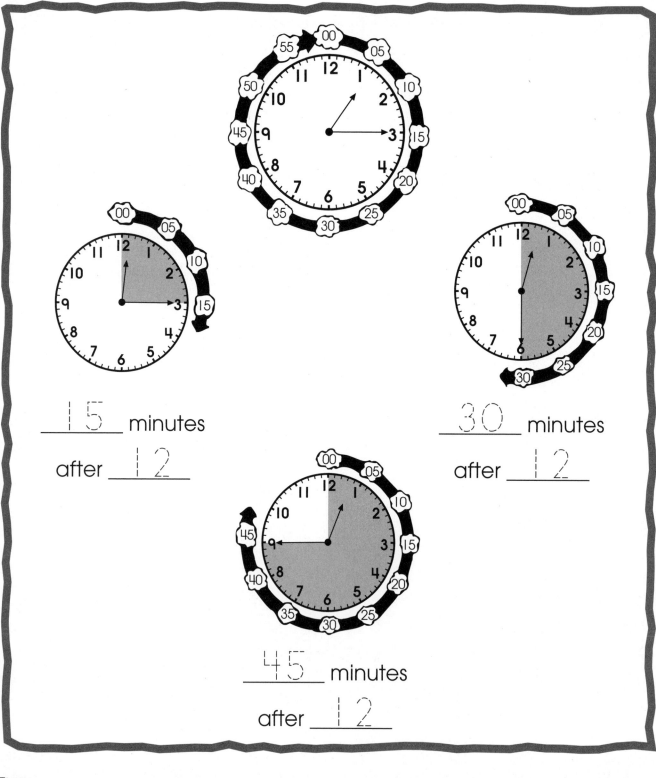

_15_ minutes

after _12_

_30_ minutes

after _12_

_45_ minutes

after _12_

Name _____

Circle the correct digital time.

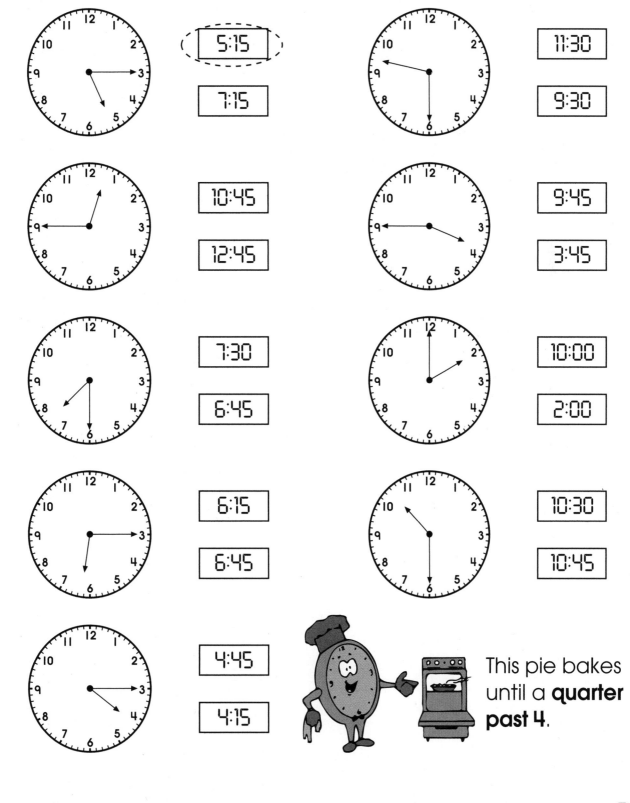

5:15

7:15

11:30

9:30

10:45

12:45

9:45

3:45

7:30

6:45

10:00

2:00

6:15

6:45

10:30

10:45

4:45

4:15

This pie bakes until a **quarter past 4**.

Time

Money

Name _____

It is important to learn about money.

This is a **penny**.

It is worth **1 cent**. It has 2 sides.

This is the **cent symbol. Trace** it.

¢
_____

Color the pennies **brown**.

Name _____

Count the pennies in each row. ✏️ **Write** how much.

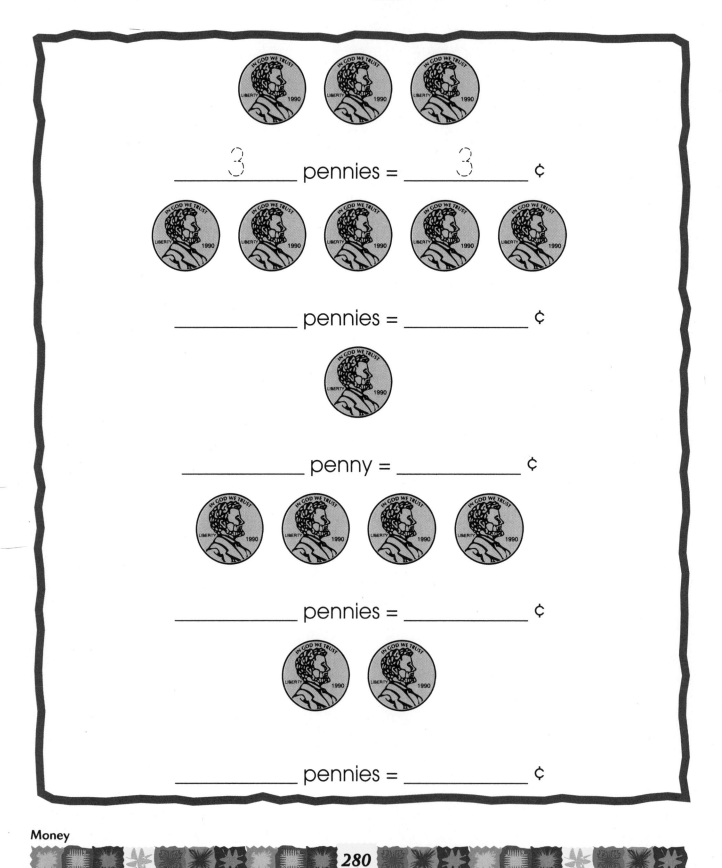

_____3_____ pennies = _____3_____ ¢

_____ pennies = _____ ¢

_____ penny = _____ ¢

_____ pennies = _____ ¢

_____ pennies = _____ ¢

Name _____

Look at Henny Penny's eggs.

I penny   I cent

✏️ **Write** how much money.

Example:

= 5 ¢

= ▢ ¢

= ▢ ¢

= ▢ ¢

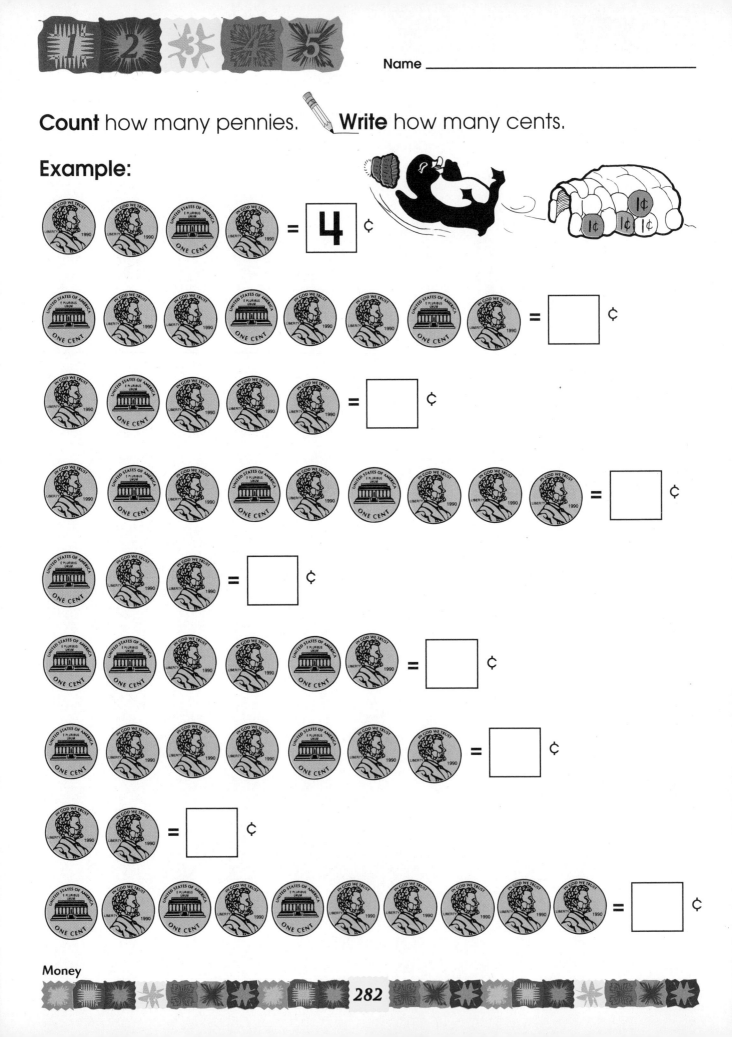

Count how many pennies. **Write** how many cents.

Example:

= **4** ¢

= ☐ ¢

= ☐ ¢

= ☐ ¢

= ☐ ¢

= ☐ ¢

= ☐ ¢

= ☐ ¢

= ☐ ¢

Name _____

Count the pennies on the flowers. **Write** the cents in the center.

Money

Name _____

Count the pennies in each chain. ✏️ **Draw** a line to the number of pennies.

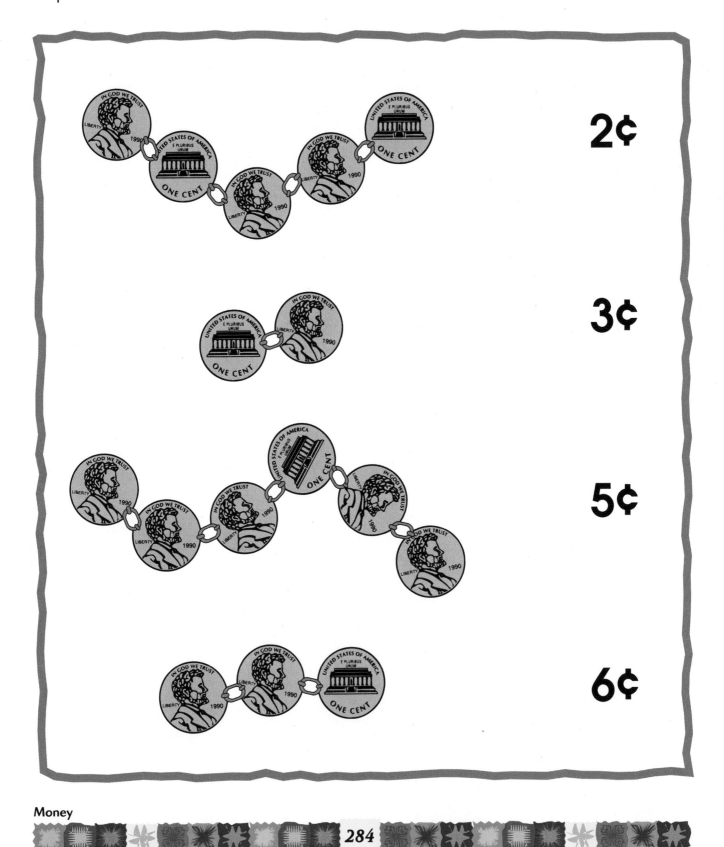

2¢

3¢

5¢

6¢

Look at the penny pinchers. **Draw** a line from the pennies to the right numbers.

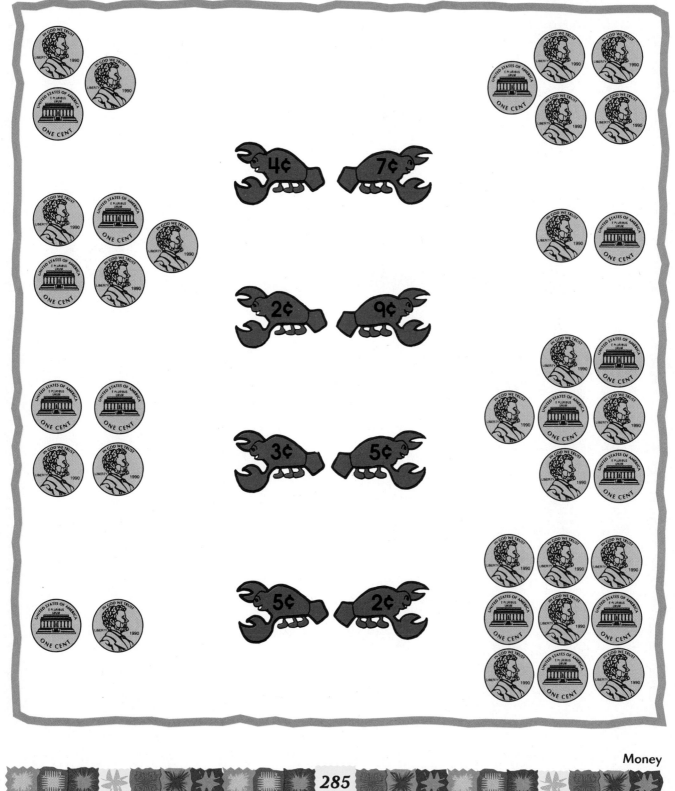

Money

Name _____

I put my pennies in bags. **Write** the number of pennies on each bag. **Color** each penny.

Money

Name _____

Count the pennies in each triangle. **Write** the amount.

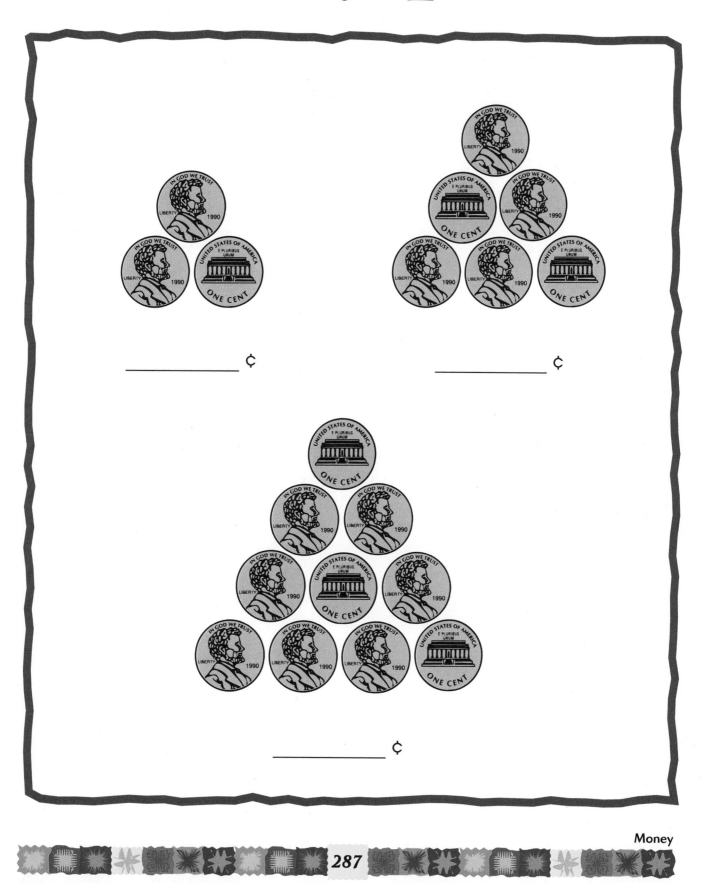

_____ ¢

_____ ¢

_____ ¢

Who has more money? **Count** the money. **Write** the amount.

_____ ¢

_____ ¢

Circle the answer.

Name _____

Meet the nickel. Look at the two sides of a nickel. ✏️ **Trace** the numbers and **write** the number of the cents in the bottom row. **Color** the nickels **silver**.

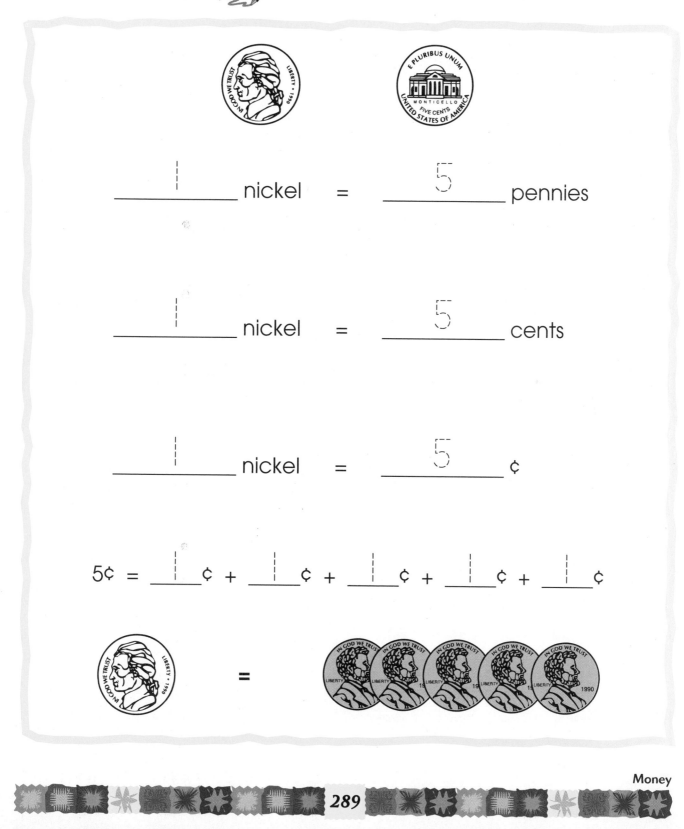

_____ 1 _____ nickel = _____ 5 _____ pennies

_____ 1 _____ nickel = _____ 5 _____ cents

_____ 1 _____ nickel = _____ 5 _____ ¢

5¢ = ___1___ ¢ + ___1___ ¢ + ___1___ ¢ + ___1___ ¢ + ___1___ ¢

Name _____

Let's **count** the nickels to see if there are enough to buy something!
Count by 5's. See how far you can count.

___5___, ___10___, ___15___, ___20___, ___25___,

___30___, ___35___, ___40___, ___45___, ___50___,

___55___, ___60___, ___65___, ___70___, ___75___,

___80___, ___85___, ___90___, ___95___, ___100___,

That is how you count nickels!

Practice counting by 5's!

Money

Name _____

Each **nickel** is worth **5 cents**. **Write** how much these nickels are worth. Remember to count by 5's.

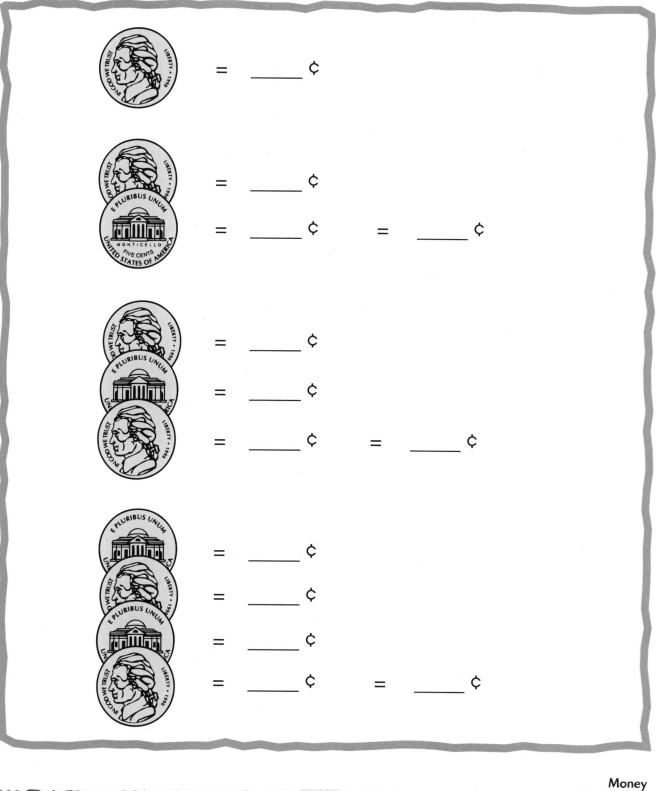

Name _____

You can buy these pickles for a nickel. **Count** the nickels by 5's.
 Write the amount.

5 cents = 1 nickel

PICKLES 5¢ each

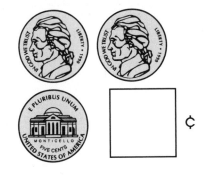 ¢

Count __5__, __10__, __15__.

Count ____, ____. ¢

Count ____, ____, ____,
____, ____.

Count ____, ____, ____, ____,
____, ____.

 ¢

Count ____, ____,
____, ____.

 ¢

Count ____, ____, ____,
____, ____, ____.

Money

How much money is in each hive of five? Count by 5's and write the amount of money.

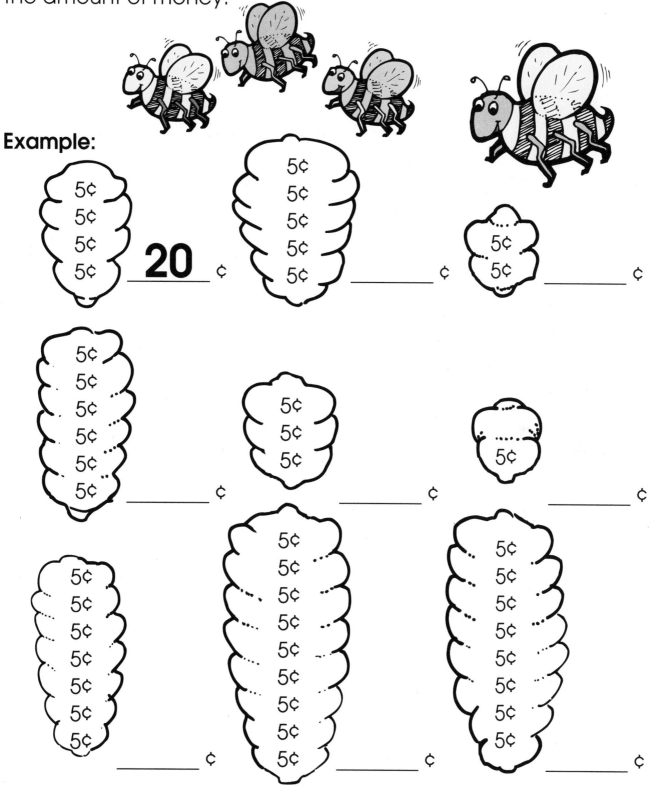

Example:

5¢
5¢
5¢
5¢
20 ¢

5¢
5¢
5¢
5¢
5¢
_____ ¢

5¢
5¢
_____ ¢

5¢
5¢
5¢
5¢
5¢
5¢
_____ ¢

5¢
5¢
5¢
_____ ¢

5¢
_____ ¢

5¢
5¢
5¢
5¢
5¢
5¢
5¢
_____ ¢

5¢
5¢
5¢
5¢
5¢
5¢
5¢
5¢
5¢
_____ ¢

5¢
5¢
5¢
5¢
5¢
5¢
5¢
5¢
_____ ¢

Money

Name _____

Look at the price on each toy. **Color** it if there are enough nickels to buy it.

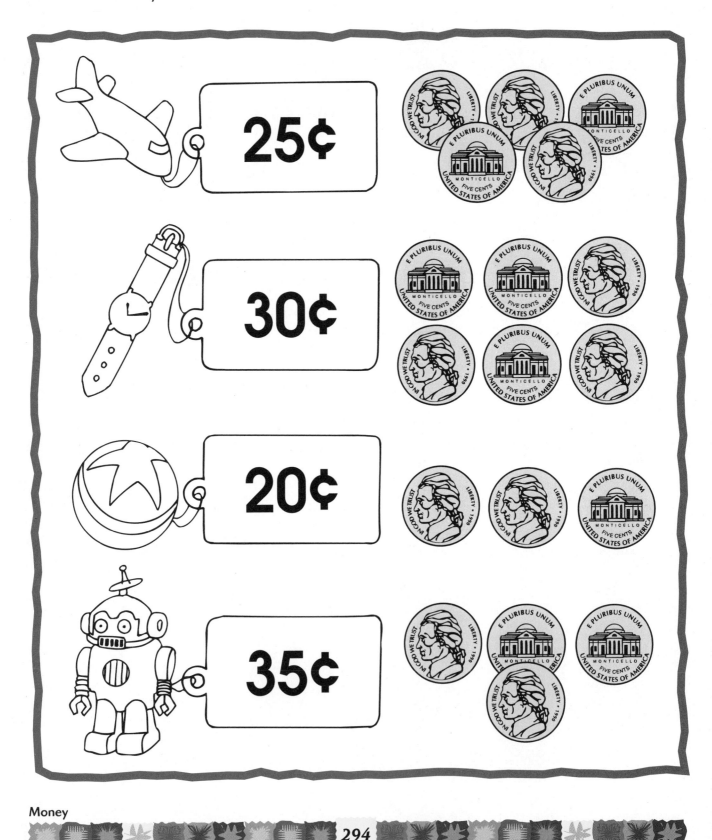

Name _____

Count the nickels. **Write** the amount of money in each meter.

Example:

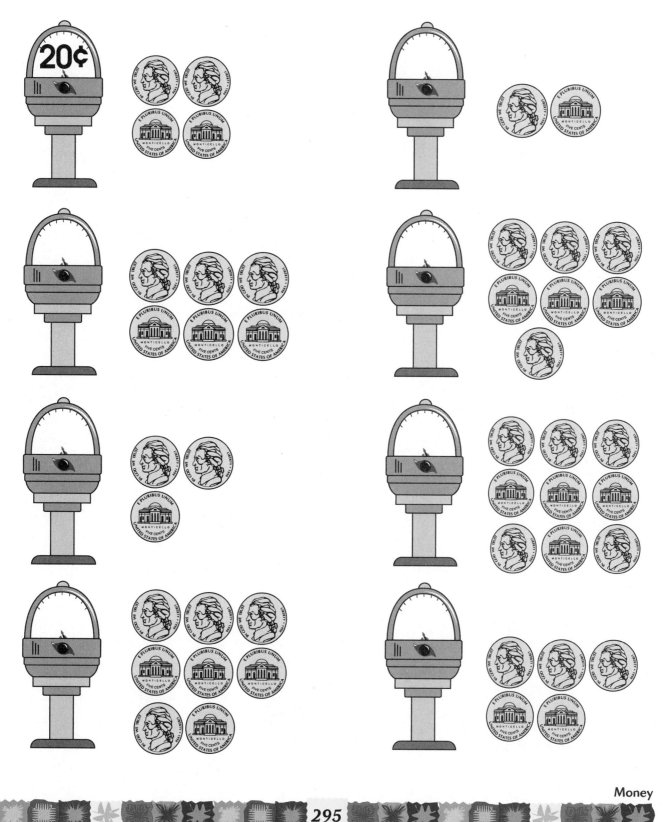

Name _____

Count by 5's. **Color** the correct number of nickels for each bag. Begin at the star. Watch out for the pennies!

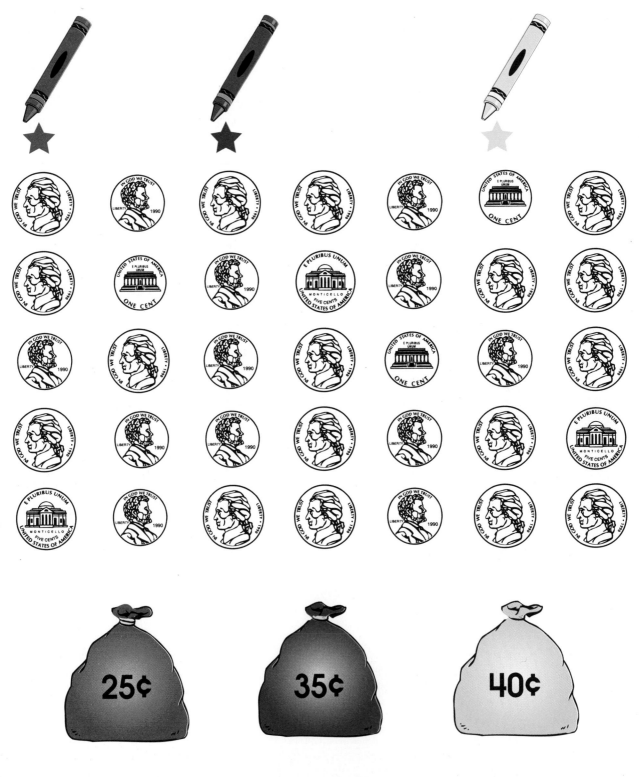

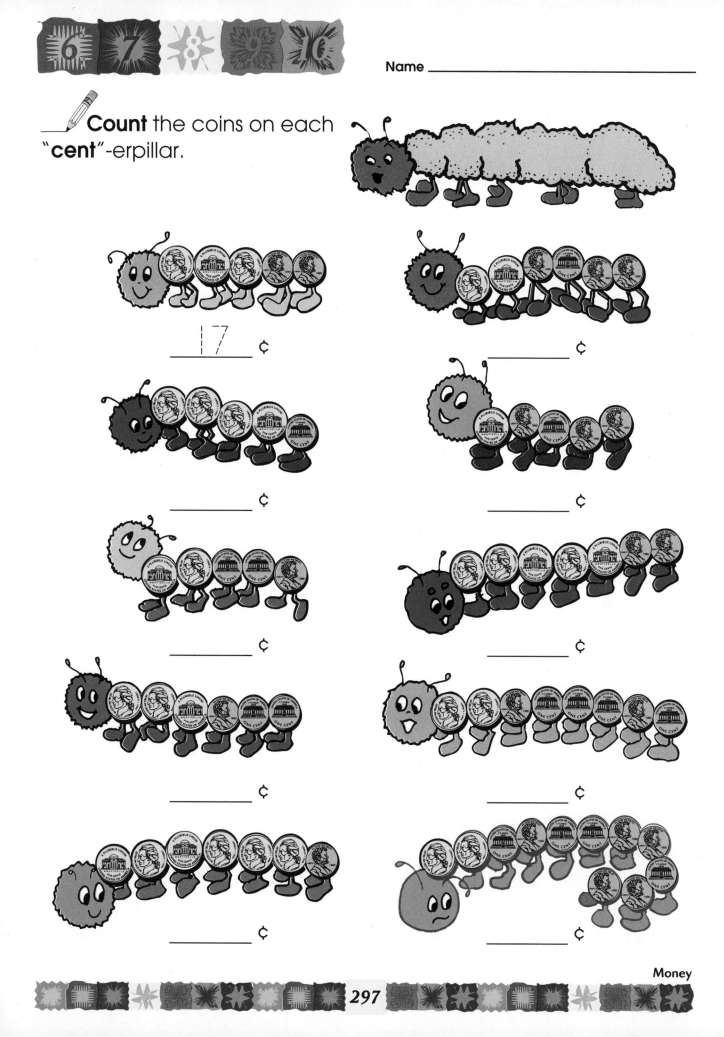

Count the coins on each "**cent**"-erpillar.

17 ¢

_____ ¢

_____ ¢

_____ ¢

_____ ¢

_____ ¢

_____ ¢

_____ ¢

_____ ¢

_____ ¢

Name _____

Count the coins. ✏️ **Write** numbers in the blanks to complete the addition sentences.

$\underline{5}$ ¢ + $\underline{1}$ ¢ = _____

_____ ¢ + _____ ¢ = _____

_____ ¢ + _____ ¢ = _____

_____ ¢ + _____ ¢ = _____

_____ ¢ + _____ ¢ = _____

Name _____

You have met the penny and the nickel. Now, meet the dime!
A dime is small, but quite strong. It can buy more than a penny
or a nickel.

front

back

Each side of a dime is different. It has ridges on its edge. **Color**
the dime **silver**.

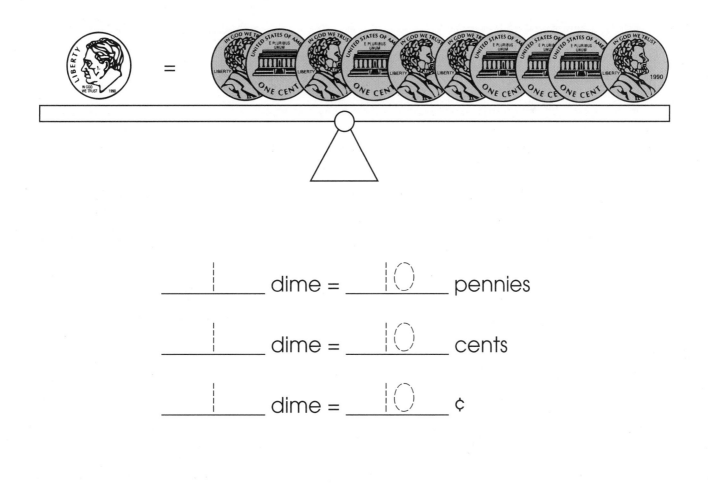

_____1_____ dime = _____10_____ pennies

_____1_____ dime = _____10_____ cents

_____1_____ dime = _____10_____ ¢

Name _____

Count by 10's. ✏ **Write** the number. ✏ **Circle** the group with more.

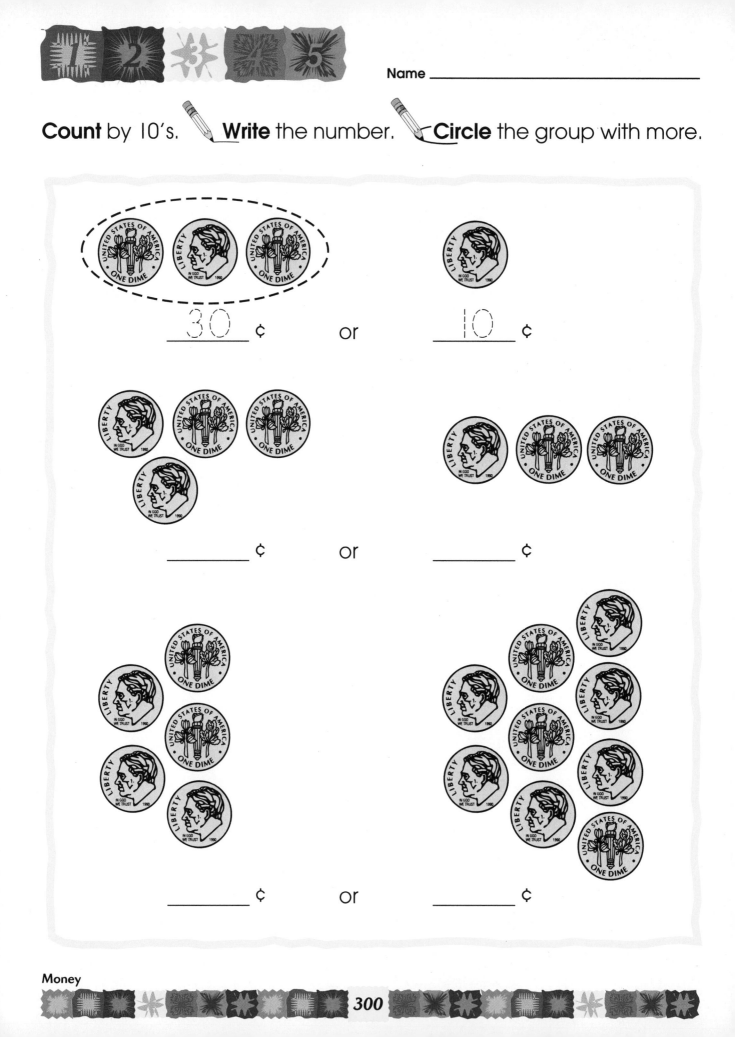

___30___ ¢   or   ___10___ ¢

_____ ¢   or   _____ ¢

_____ ¢   or   _____ ¢

Name _____

Count the dimes and the pennies.

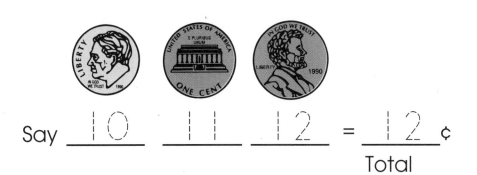

Say ___10___ ___11___ ___12___ = ___12___ ¢

Total

Begin with the dime, then **add** the pennies.
Write the amount.

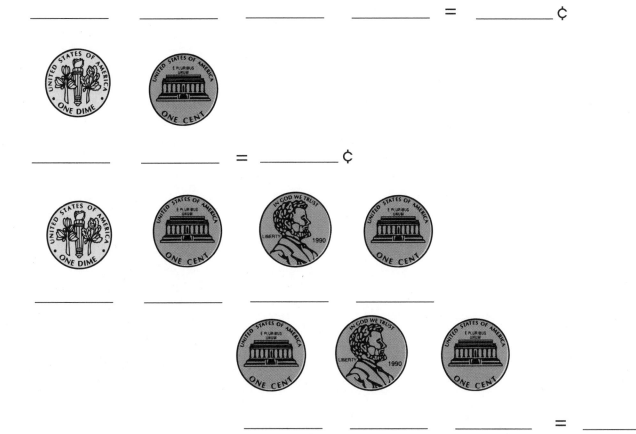

_____ _____ _____ _____ = _____ ¢

_____ _____ = _____ ¢

_____

_____ _____ = _____ ¢

Name _____

Count the money. **Count** the dimes, then **count** the nickels. **Write** the amount.

_____ ¢   _____ ¢   _____ ¢   _____ ¢   _____ ¢   _____ ¢
                                                                Total

_____ ¢   _____ ¢   _____ ¢   _____ ¢   _____ ¢   _____ ¢

_____ ¢   _____ ¢   _____ ¢   _____ ¢
                                    Total

Solve this puzzle.

What coins does Raccoon have?
Draw them here.

I'm counting my money.
10¢, 20¢, 30¢, 35¢,
40¢, 45¢, 50¢...

Money

Name _____

Count the dimes, nickels, and pennies. **Write** how many cents.

_____ ¢

_____ ¢

_____ ¢

If you add 1 more penny to the
first row, you will have _____ ¢

If you add 1 more penny to the
second row, you will have _____ ¢

If you add 1 more penny to the
third row, you will have _____ ¢

**To count these cents
takes a lot of sense!**

Money

Name _____

Count the money. Start with dimes. Then count the nickels and pennies. ✏️ **Write** your answer on the "Total" line.

_____ ¢   _____ ¢   _____ ¢   _____ ¢   _____ ¢   _____ ¢

Total

_____ ¢   _____ ¢   _____ ¢   _____ ¢

_____ ¢   _____ ¢   _____ ¢   _____ ¢

Total

Money

Name _____

Count the money. ✏️ **Write** each amount on the line.

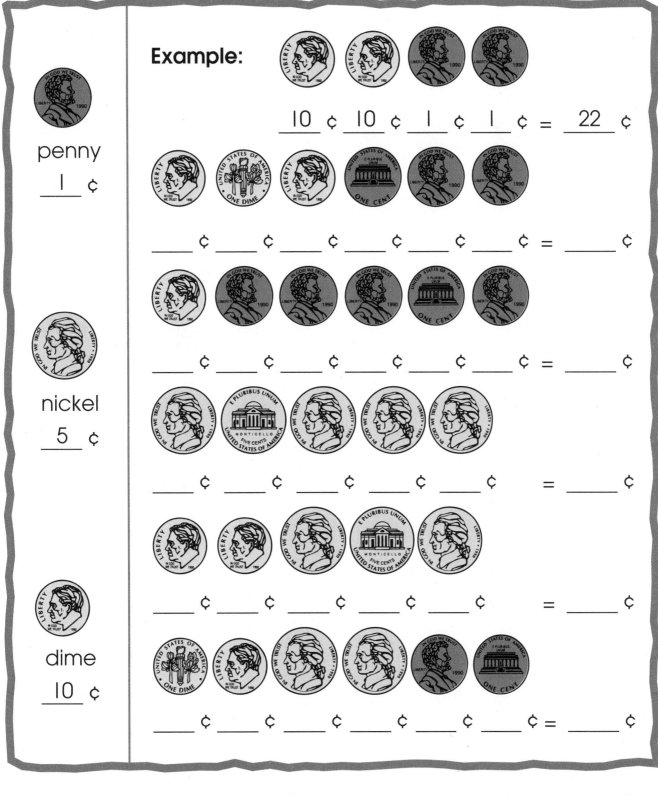

penny
__1__ ¢

nickel
__5__ ¢

dime
__10__ ¢

Example:

__10__ ¢ __10__ ¢ __1__ ¢ __1__ ¢ = __22__ ¢

____ ¢ ____ ¢ ____ ¢ ____ ¢ ____ ¢ ____ ¢ = ____ ¢

____ ¢ ____ ¢ ____ ¢ ____ ¢ ____ ¢ ____ ¢ = ____ ¢

____ ¢ ____ ¢ ____ ¢ ____ ¢ ____ ¢ = ____ ¢

____ ¢ ____ ¢ ____ ¢ ____ ¢ ____ ¢ = ____ ¢

____ ¢ ____ ¢ ____ ¢ ____ ¢ ____ ¢ ____ ¢ = ____ ¢

Money

There is a bake sale at school today. Take some money with you!

Decide which one you want. In the space below, **draw** enough money to pay for it.

Name _____

At the bake sale, Sharita chose the doughnut. Look at the previous page.

✏️ **Circle** the money she needed.

   _____ ¢

Robert loves brownies.

✏️ **Circle** the money he needed.

   _____ ¢

Tom had 3 of these.

He had _____ ¢. He spent it all on something good. ✏️ **Draw** it here.

Money

Name _____

Here is a **quarter**. Our first President, George Washington, is on the **front**. The American eagle is on the **back**.

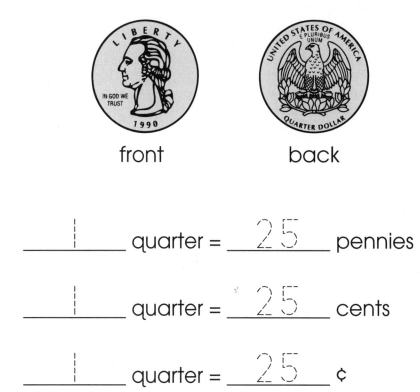

front   back

_____1_____ quarter = ___25___ pennies

_____1_____ quarter = ___25___ cents

_____1_____ quarter = ___25___ ¢

Count these nickels by 5's. Is this another way to make 25¢?
 Circle "yes" or "no."

yes   no

Money

Name _____

These are all ways to make **25¢**.
Color each coin.

I quarter

5 nickels

2 dimes,
I nickel

25
pennies

Name _____

It cost 25¢ to catch a fish. Circle each group of coins that makes 25¢. Do not circle any coin more than once. How many fish can I catch?

Draw and **color** the number of fish I can catch.

Name _____

Patty bought these pears at the store. She paid **25¢** for each pear. **Color** the pears.

25¢ each

Draw the quarters she spent.

How much did she spend? _____ ¢

Jennifer bought these bananas. She paid **10¢** for each one. **Color** the bananas.

10¢ each

Draw the dimes she spent.

How much money did she spend? _____ ¢

Which girl spent less? _____

Money

Name _____

Count the money. **Write** the amount. A **quarter** is worth **25¢**.

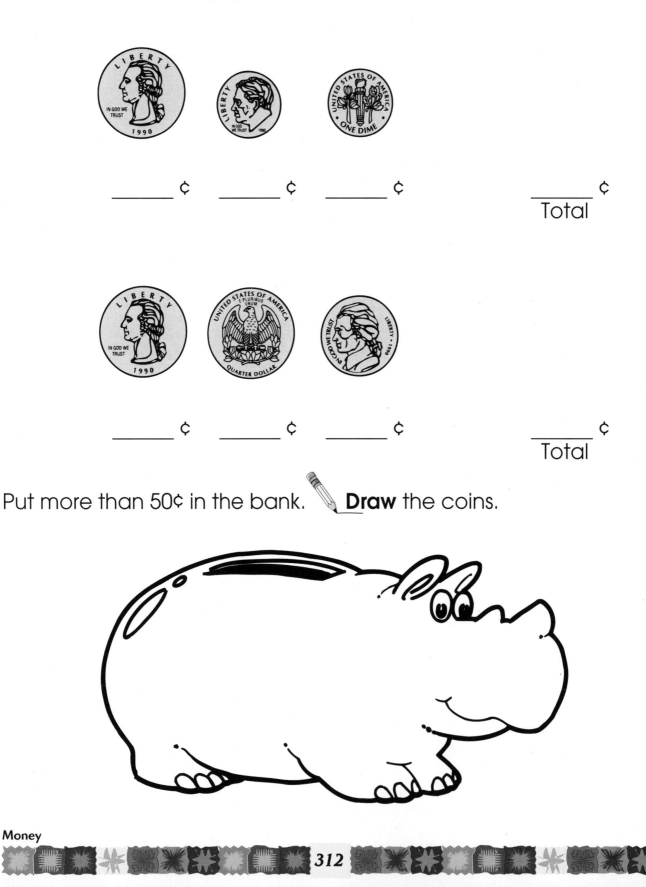

_____ ¢   _____ ¢   _____ ¢   _____ ¢
                                                    Total

_____ ¢   _____ ¢   _____ ¢   _____ ¢
                                                    Total

Put more than 50¢ in the bank. **Draw** the coins.

Name _____

Count the money. Start with the quarters. Then **count** the dimes, nickels, and pennies.

_____ ¢   _____ ¢   _____ ¢   _____ ¢   _____ ¢   _____ ¢
                                                                          Total

_____ ¢   _____ ¢   _____ ¢   _____ ¢   _____ ¢   _____ ¢

_____ ¢   _____ ¢   _____ ¢
                              Total

Solve this puzzle. What coins does Lizard have? **Write** the number of each coin.

_____

_____

I'm counting my money. 25¢, 35¢, 45¢, 55¢, 60¢, 65¢, 66¢, 67¢.

Count the coins. Start with the quarters. ✏️ **Write** the amount in each football.

45¢

¢

¢

¢

¢

¢

Number Rhymes
and Activities

For Parents, Caregivers, and Educators:

This section includes songs, rhymes, and activities for children that teach and reinforce numbers to 100 in creative and playful ways. You may wish to sing the rhyme to a familiar tune to make learning easier and more fun, or have the children make up a tune together.

There are several counting activities for each number through 10. The songs, rhymes, and activities include a variety of curriculum areas such as language, math, music, and movement. Many of these activities can serve as springboards to other ideas; that is, you may think of another or better way of presenting a certain number. Encourage the children to follow along while you read, and act out the activity. For example, for "Five Little Cookies," you may wish to use five flannel cookie shapes on a flannel board and have children take away one "cookie" at a time as you say the verse. Children will also enjoy acting out "Bears on the Train."

If some of the activities appear to be too juvenile for the children that you are working with, encourage them to lead a younger sibling or friend with the verses. This will help reinforce numbers and counting for the child leading the activities.

Although these songs, rhymes, and activities are educational, they are also fun. Enjoy each activity with the children as you work with them to learn their numbers and counting.

Five Little Cookies

Five little cookies by the door

Mother ate one.
Now there are four.

Four little cookies by the tree

Father ate one.
Now there are three.

Three little cookies by the shoe

Sister ate one.
Now there are two.

Two little cookies just got done

Brother ate one.
Now there is one.

One little cookie, the only one

I ate it.
Now there are none.

Name _____

Six Days of Summer

On the first day
of summer,
What did I see?

A robin up in a tree.

On the second day
of summer,
What did I see?

Two ducks swimming
And a robin up in a tree.

On the third day
of summer,
What did I see?

Three bees buzzing,
Two ducks swimming,
And a robin up in a tree.

On the fourth day of summer,
What did I see?

Four dogs barking, three bees buzzing,
Two ducks swimming,
And a robin up in a tree.

Name _____

On the fifth day of summer
What did I see?

Five picnic baskets, four dogs barking,
Three bees buzzing,
Two ducks swimming,
And a robin up in a tree.

On the sixth day of summer
What did I see?

Six flowers growing, five picnic baskets,
Four dogs barking, three bees buzzing,
Two ducks swimming,
And a robin up in a tree.

Ten Little Bunnies

Ten little bunnies jumping on the bed,

One fell off and bumped her head.
How many bunnies
Jumping on the bed? _____

Nine little bunnies jumping on the bed,

One fell off and bumped his head.
How many bunnies
Jumping on the bed? _____

Eight little bunnies jumping on the bed,

One fell off and bumped her head.
How many bunnies
Jumping on the bed? _____

Seven little bunnies jumping on the bed,

One fell off and bumped his head.
How many bunnies
Jumping on the bed? _____

Six little bunnies jumping on the bed,

One fell off and bumped her head.
How many bunnies
Jumping on the bed? _____

Five little bunnies jumping on the bed,

One fell off and bumped his head.
How many bunnies
Jumping on the bed? _____

Four little bunnies jumping on the bed,

One fell off and bumped her head.
How many bunnies
Jumping on the bed? _____

Three little bunnies jumping on the bed,

One fell off and bumped his head.
How many bunnies
Jumping on the bed? _____

Two little bunnies jumping on the bed,

One fell off and bumped her head.
How many bunnies
Jumping on the bed? _____

One little bunny jumping on the bed,

He fell off and bumped his head.
How many bunnies
Jumping on the bed? _____

Ten little bunnies lying on the floor.
"Get back to bed and jump no more!"

Boots for Sale

How many boots
should the little duck buy
To keep his feet
nice and dry? _____

Two little boots is
what he should buy
To keep his feet
nice and dry.

How many boots
should the little cat buy
To keep her feet
nice and dry? _____

Four little boots is
what she should buy
To keep her feet
nice and dry.

How many boots
should the little ant buy
To keep his feet
nice and dry? _____

Six little boots is
what he should buy
To keep his feet
nice and dry.

How many boots
should the little pig buy
To keep her feet
nice and dry? _____

Four little boots is
what she should buy
To keep her feet
nice and dry.

How many boots
should the little crab buy
To keep his feet
nice and dry? _____

Eight little boots is
what he should buy
To keep his feet
nice and dry.

How many boots
should the little fish buy
To keep her feet
nice and dry? _____

Zero little boots is
what she should buy
To keep her feet
nice and dry.

Bears on the Train

Ten little bears riding on the train
Looks like it is going to rain.

Two little bears get off the train.
How many bears are now
Riding on the train? _____

Eight little bears riding on the train
Looks like it is going to rain.

Two more bears get off the train.
How many bears are now
Riding on the train? _____

Six little bears riding on the train
Looks like it is going to rain.

Two more bears get off the train.
How many bears are now
Riding on the train? _____

Four little bears riding on the train
Looks like it is going to rain.

Two more bears get off the train.
How many bears are now
Riding on the train?

Two little bears riding on the train
Looks like it is going to rain.

Two more bears get off the train.
How many bears are now
Riding on the train? _____

Zero bears riding on the train
Crash! Boom!
Down comes the rain!

On the Pond

One little girl rowing in the pond,

Another girl comes along.
How many girls are now
Rowing in the pond? _____

Two little birds flying over the pond,

Two more birds come along.
How many birds are now
Flying over the pond? _____

Three little fish
Swimming in the pond,

Another fish comes along.
How many fish are now
Swimming in the pond? _____

Four little ducks
Swimming in the pond,

Another duck comes along.
How many ducks are now
Swimming in the pond? _____

Five little butterflies
Flying over the pond,

Another butterfly comes along.
How many butterflies are now
Flying over the pond? _____

Challenge:

How many are there altogether? _____

Answer Key

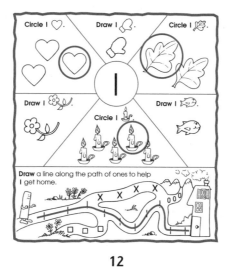

12

13

14

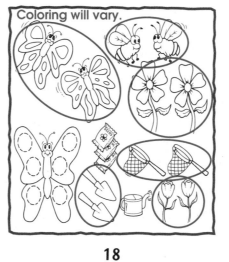

18

19

20

24

25

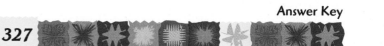

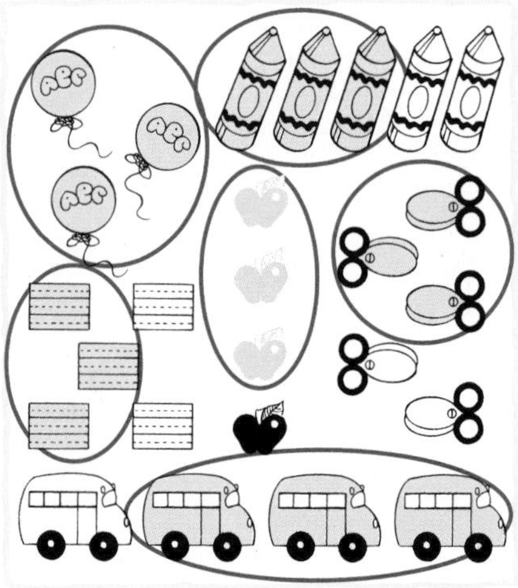

26

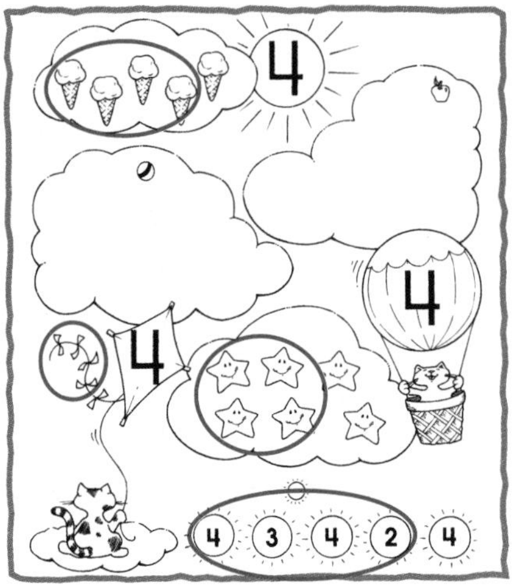

30

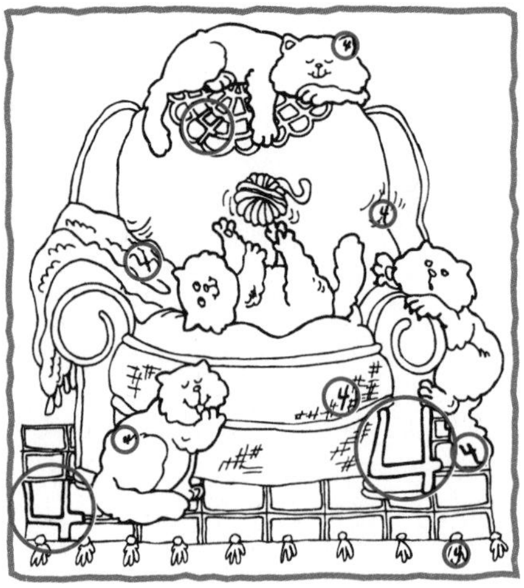

31

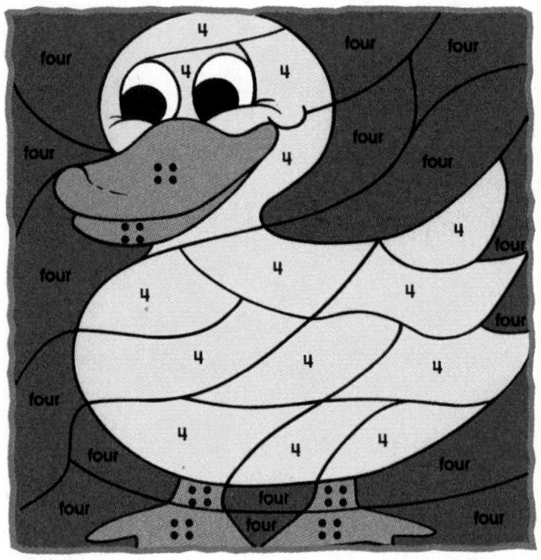

32

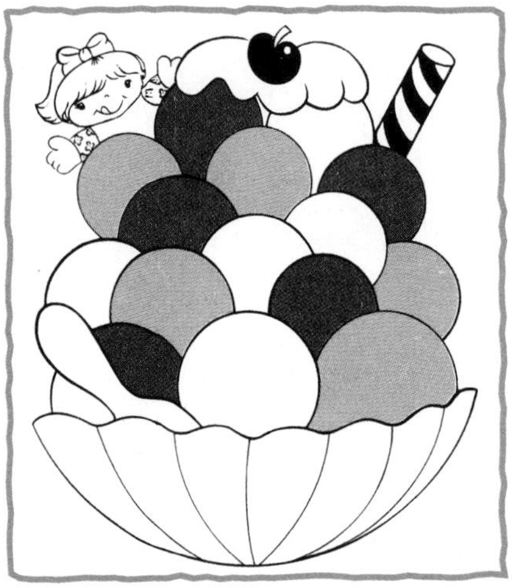

36

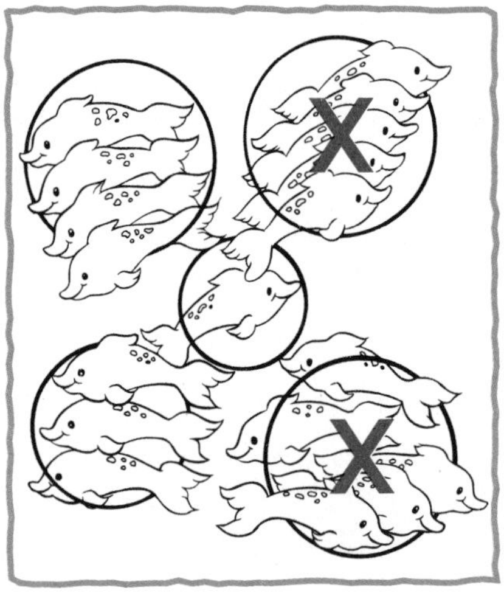

37

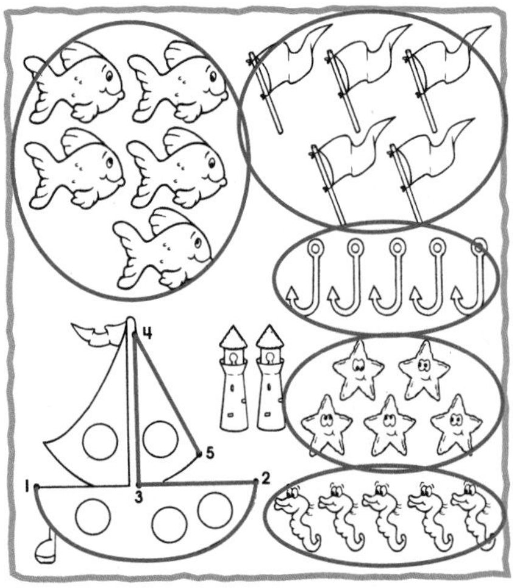

38

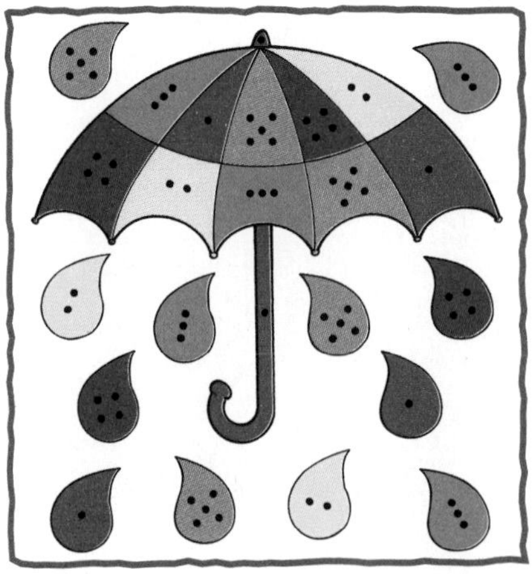

40

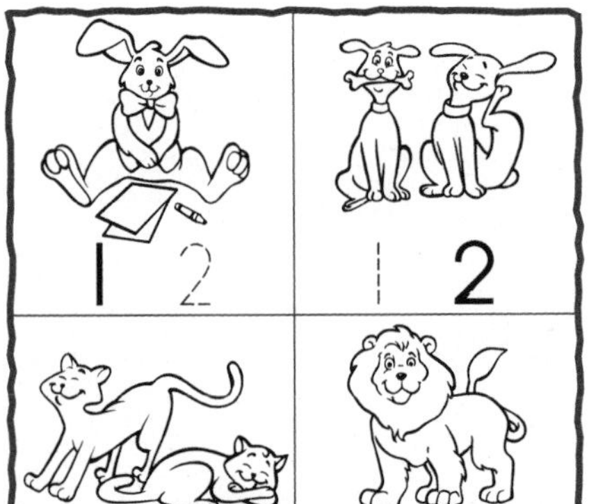

41

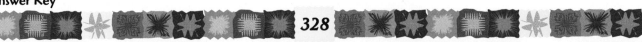

42

43

44

45

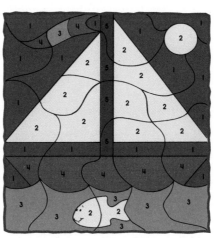

46

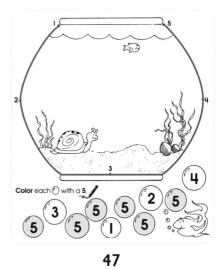

47

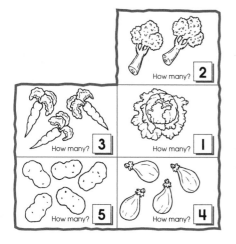

48

49

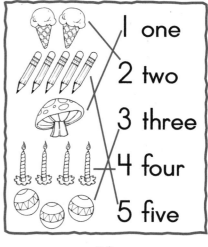

50

51

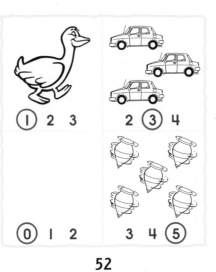

52

53

54

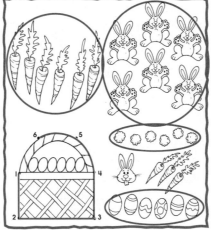

58

59

How many 🐰? **6**

60

How many 🐸? **7**

64

65

Answer Key

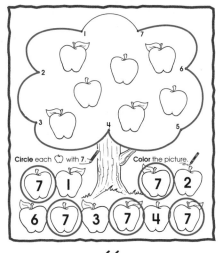

66

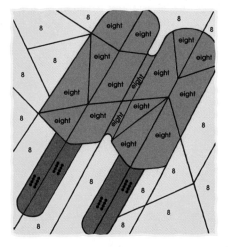

70

71

75

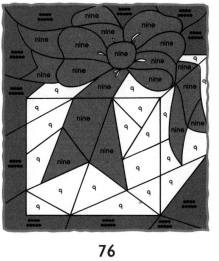

76

80

81

84

85

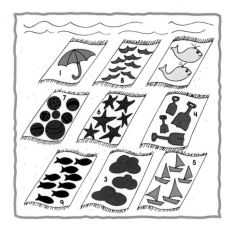

86

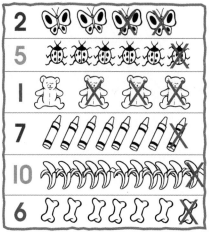

87

88

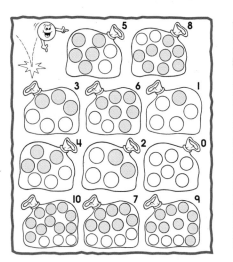

89

90

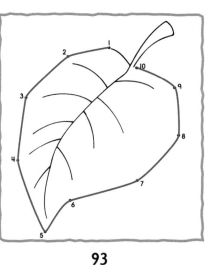

91

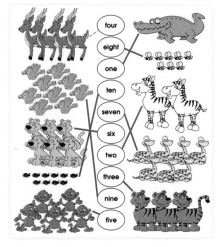

92

93

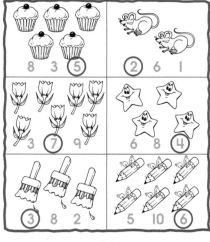

94

95

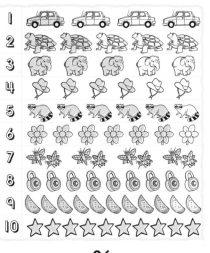

96

97

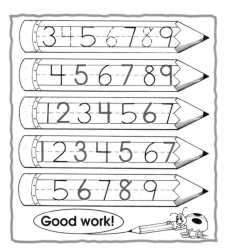

98

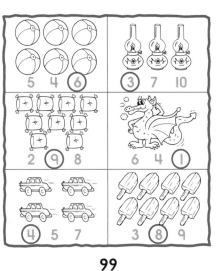

99

100

101

102

103

Answer Key

107

111

112

116

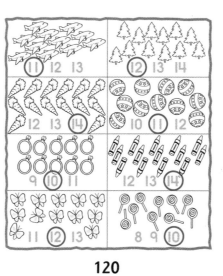

120

124

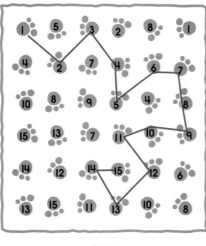

125

129

133

137

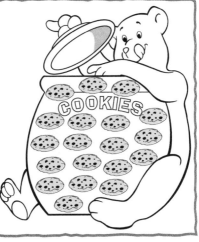

141

145

148

149

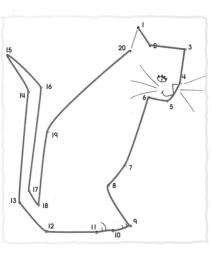

150

151

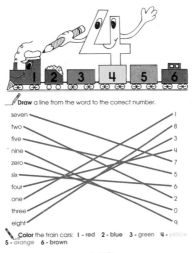

152

153

Answer Key

154

155

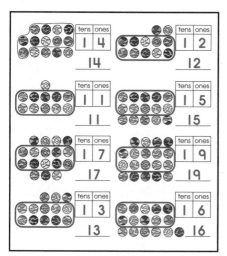

158

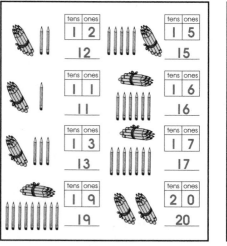

159

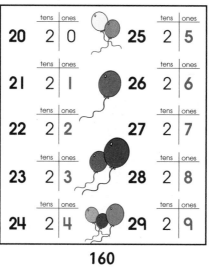

160

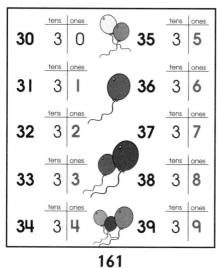

161

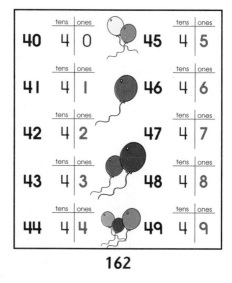

162

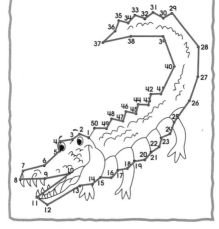

164

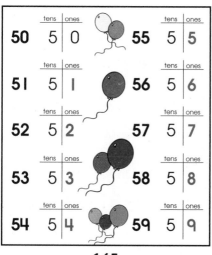

165

Answer Key

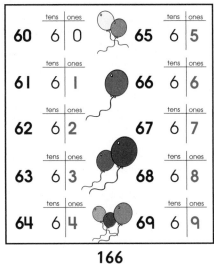

60	6	0
61	6	1
62	6	2
63	6	3
64	6	4

65	6	5
66	6	6
67	6	7
68	6	8
69	6	9

166

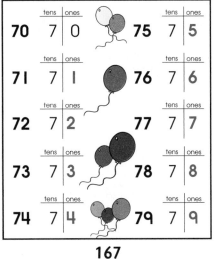

70	7	0
71	7	1
72	7	2
73	7	3
74	7	4

75	7	5
76	7	6
77	7	7
78	7	8
79	7	9

167

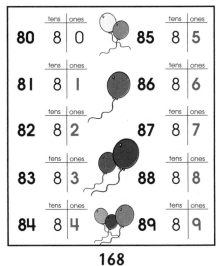

80	8	0
81	8	1
82	8	2
83	8	3
84	8	4

85	8	5
86	8	6
87	8	7
88	8	8
89	8	9

168

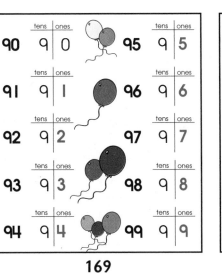

90	9	0
91	9	1
92	9	2
93	9	3
94	9	4

95	9	5
96	9	6
97	9	7
98	9	8
99	9	9

169

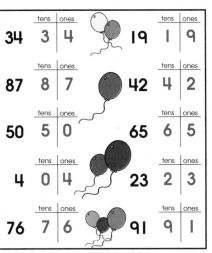

34	3	4
87	8	7
50	5	0
4	0	4
76	7	6

19	1	9
42	4	2
65	6	5
23	2	3
91	9	1

170

35   3 tens   5 ones
19   1 tens   9 ones
8   0 tens   8 ones
26   2 tens   6 ones
49   4 tens   9 ones
10   1 tens   0 ones

4 tens 6 ones 46   3 tens 2 ones 32
2 tens 9 ones 29   4 tens 0 ones 40
1 ten 4 ones   14   0 tens 6 ones 6
2 tens 1 one   21   4 tens 7 ones 47
3 tens 3 ones 33   1 ten 1 one   11

171

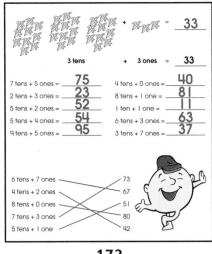

3 tens + 3 ones = 33

7 tens + 5 ones = 75   4 tens + 0 ones = 40
2 tens + 3 ones = 23   8 tens + 1 one = 81
5 tens + 2 ones = 52   1 ten + 1 one = 11
5 tens + 4 ones = 54   6 tens + 3 ones = 63
9 tens + 5 ones = 95   3 tens + 7 ones = 37

6 tens + 7 ones ——— 73
4 tens + 2 ones ——— 67
8 tens + 0 ones ——— 51
7 tens + 3 ones ——— 80
5 tens + 1 one ——— 42

172

174

175

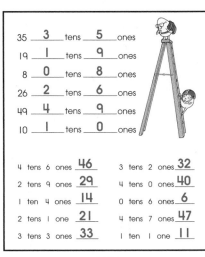

Answer Key

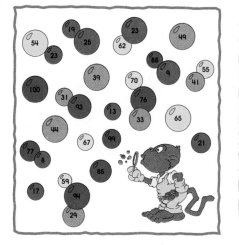

176

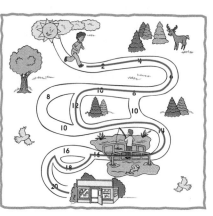

178

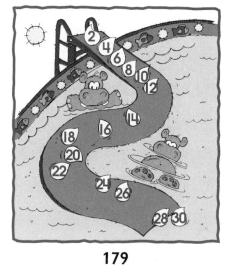

179

WELL BE
CROAKING
ROUND THE
BACKYARD

180

181

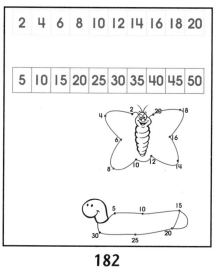

2	4	6	8	10	12	14	16	18	20

5	10	15	20	25	30	35	40	45	50

182

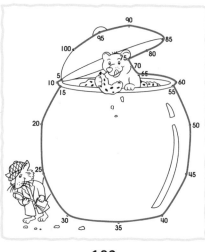

183

184

185

186

1 2 3 4 (5) 6 7 8 9 (10)
11 12 13 14 (15) 16 17 18 19 (20)
21 22 23 24 (25) 26 27 28 29 (30)
31 32 33 34 (35) 36 37 38 39 (40)
41 42 43 44 (45) 46 47 48 49 (50)

_5_ _10_ _15_ _20_ _25_ _30_ _35_ _40_
_45_ _50_

1 2 3 4 5 6 7 8 9 [10]
11 12 13 14 15 16 17 18 19 [20]
21 22 23 24 25 26 27 28 29 [30]
31 32 33 34 35 36 37 38 39 [40]
41 42 43 44 45 46 47 48 49 [50]

_10_ _20_ _30_ _40_ _50_

187

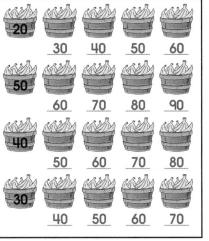

20 _30_ _40_ _50_ _60_
50 _60_ _70_ _80_ _90_
40 _50_ _60_ _70_ _80_
30 _40_ _50_ _60_ _70_

188

2 4 6 8 10
12 14 16 18 20

5 10 15 20 25
30 35 40 45 50

10 20 30 40 50
60 70 80 90 100

189

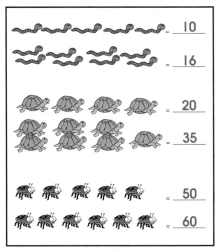

= 10
= 16
= 20
= 35
= 50
= 60

190

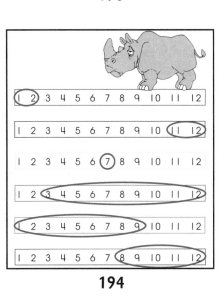

① ② ③ ④ ⑤ ⑥ ❼ ⑧

191

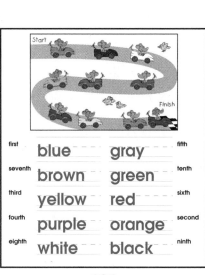

first — blue   gray — fifth
seventh — brown   green — tenth
third — yellow   red — sixth
fourth — purple   orange — second
eighth — white   black — ninth

192

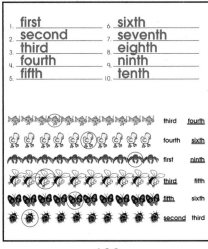

1. first   6. sixth
2. second   7. seventh
3. third   8. eighth
4. fourth   9. ninth
5. fifth   10. tenth

third _fourth_
fourth _sixth_
first _ninth_
third fifth
fifth sixth
second third

194

(1 2) 3 4 5 6 7 8 9 10 11 12
1 2 3 4 5 6 7 8 9 10 (11 12)
1 2 3 4 5 6 (7) 8 9 10 11 12
1 2 (3 4 5 6 7 8 9 10 11 12)
1 (2 3 4 5 6 7 8 9) 10 11 12
1 2 3 4 5 6 7 (8 9 10 11 12)

195

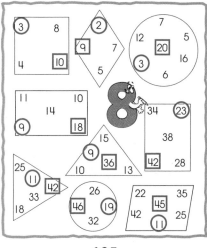

3 8 (2) 7 7
9 7 12 5
4 10 5 [20] 16
(3) 6

11 10 34 (23)
14 38
(9) 18 15 42 28
9 36 13

25 26
(11) 42 (46) (19) 22 35
33 32 45
18 42 25
(11)

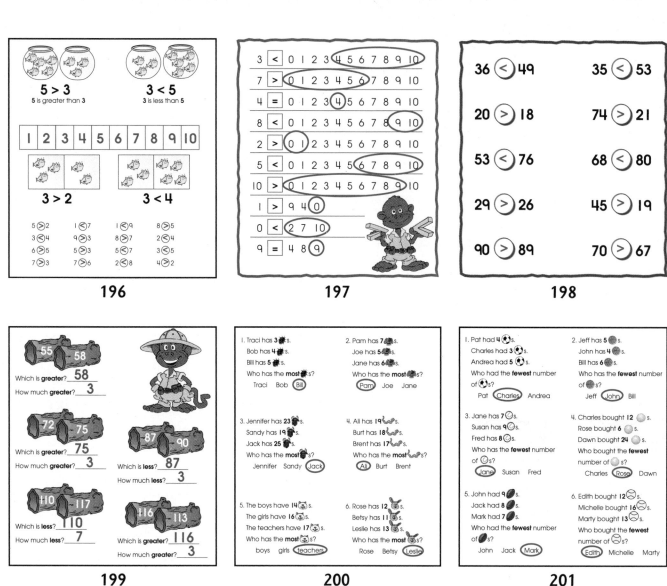

196

5 > 3 — 5 is greater than 3
3 < 5 — 3 is less than 5

1 2 3 4 5 6 7 8 9 10

3 > 2   3 < 4

5 > 2	1 < 7
3 < 4	9 > 3
6 > 5	5 > 3
7 > 3	7 > 6

1 < 9	8 > 5
8 > 7	2 < 4
5 < 7	3 < 5
2 < 8	4 > 2

197

3 < 0 1 2 3 (4 5 6 7 8 9 10)
7 > (0 1 2 3 4 5 6) 7 8 9 10
4 = 0 1 2 3 (4) 5 6 7 8 9 10
8 < 0 1 2 3 4 5 6 7 8 (9 10)
2 > (0 1) 2 3 4 5 6 7 8 9 10
5 < 0 1 2 3 4 5 (6 7 8 9 10)
10 > (0 1 2 3 4 5 6 7 8 9) 10
1 > 9 4 (0)
0 < (2 7 10)
9 = 4 8 (9)

198

36 < 49	35 < 53
20 > 18	74 > 21
53 < 76	68 < 80
29 > 26	45 > 19
90 > 89	70 > 67

199

55 58
Which is greater? 58
How much greater? 3

72 75
Which is greater? 75
How much greater? 3

87 90
Which is less? 87
How much less? 3

110 117
Which is less? 110
How much less? 7

116 113
Which is greater? 116
How much greater? 3

200

1. Traci has 3. Bob has 4. Bill has 5. Who has the **most**? (Bill)
2. Pam has 7. Joe has 5. Jane has 6. Who has the **most**? (Pam)
3. Jennifer has 23. Sandy has 19. Jack has 25. Who has the **most**? (Jack)
4. Ali has 19. Burt has 18. Brent has 17. Who has the **most**? (Ali)
5. The boys have 14. The girls have 16. The teachers have 17. Who has the **most**? (teachers)
6. Rose has 12. Betsy has 11. Leslie has 13. Who has the **most**? (Leslie)

201

1. Pat had 4. Charles had 3. Andrea had 5. Who had the **fewest** number? (Charles)
2. Jeff has 5. John has 4. Bill has 6. Who has the **fewest** number? (John)
3. Jane has 7. Susan has 9. Fred has 8. Who has the **fewest** number? (Jane)
4. Charles bought 12. Rose bought 6. Dawn bought 24. Who bought the **fewest** number? (Rose)
5. John had 9. Jack had 8. Mark had 7. Who had the **fewest** number? (Mark)
6. Edith bought 12. Michelle bought 16. Marty bought 13. Who bought the **fewest** number? (Edith)

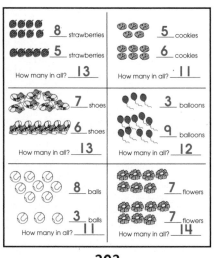

203

8 strawberries / 5 strawberries — How many in all? 13
5 cookies / 6 cookies — How many in all? 11
7 shoes / 6 shoes — How many in all? 13
3 balloons / 9 balloons — How many in all? 12
8 balls / 3 balls — How many in all? 11
7 flowers / 7 flowers — How many in all? 14

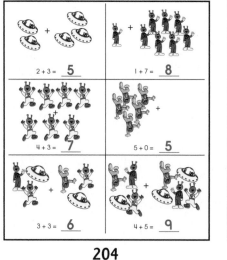

204

2 + 3 = 5	1 + 7 = 8
4 + 3 = 7	5 + 0 = 5
3 + 3 = 6	4 + 5 = 9

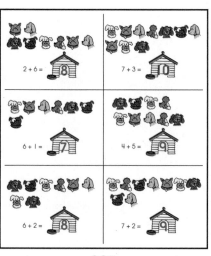

205

2 + 6 = 8	7 + 3 = 10
6 + 1 = 7	4 + 5 = 9
6 + 2 = 8	7 + 2 = 9

Answer Key

206

1 + 2 = 3 | 3 + 2 = 5
2 + 4 = 6 | 3 + 3 = 6
3 + 4 = 7 | 1 + 6 = 7

207

1 + 2 = 3 | 3 + 3 = 6
5 + 2 = 7 | 2 + 3 = 5
4 + 4 = 8 | 7 + 1 = 8

208

All petals = 7

209

210

G 5 +3 = 8	A 6 +6 = 12	T 2 +2 = 4	W 7 +6 = 13	C 3 +2 = 5
L 8 +8 = 16	R 7 +8 = 15	Y 5 +5 = 10	U 4 +3 = 7	E 9 +9 = 18
N 2 +9 = 11	O 5 +4 = 9	P 9 +8 = 17	I 6 +8 = 14	E 1 +2 = 3

YOU WILL GET AN ELECTRIC CAN OPENER

211

If 3 + 8 = 11, so does 8 + 3
If 8 + 9 = 17, so does 9 + 8
If 7 + 8 = 15, so does 8 + 7
If 4 + 6 = 10, so does 6 + 4
If 6 + 7 = 13, so does 7 + 6

212

213

3+4+2 = 9 | 5+2+1 = 8 | 2+6+3 = 11 | 5+4+2 = 11
7+3+3 = 13 | 3+1+4 = 8 | 4+6+2 = 12 | 5+2+3 = 10

214

| E 3 4 +7 = 14 | H 2 1 +9 = 12 | S 4 7 +4 = 15 | Y 7 9 +3 = 19 | A 4 5 +8 = 17 | O 7 7 +2 = 16 |
| B 9 8 +5 = 22 | P 8 4 +6 = 18 | T 9 9 +6 = 24 | I 5 2 +1 = 8 | V 6 2 +3 = 11 | R 9 6 +6 = 21 |

BOTH HAVE STRIPES

Answer Key

215

A CRUMMY MUMMY

M 7+3+1= **11**	M 7+0+2= **9**	A 6+4+5= **15**
C 5+6+3= **14**	Y 2+2+6= **10**	M 5+3+5= **13**
M 8+2+7= **17**	R 5+4+3= **12**	Y 4+2+1= **7**
U 8+3+5= **16**	M 6+2+0= **8**	U 8+1+9= **18**

216

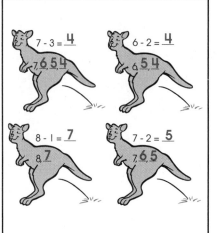

7 - 3 = **4**   6 - 2 = **4**
8 - 1 = **7**   7 - 2 = **5**

217

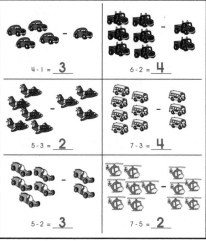

4 - 1 = **3**   6 - 2 = **4**
5 - 3 = **2**   7 - 3 = **4**
5 - 2 = **3**   7 - 5 = **2**

218

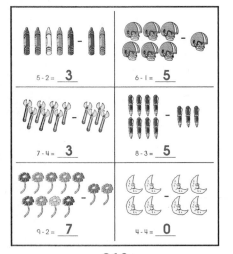

5 - 2 = **3**   6 - 1 = **5**
7 - 4 = **3**   8 - 3 = **5**
9 - 2 = **7**   4 - 4 = **0**

219

220

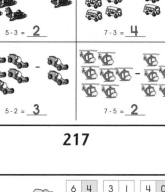

221

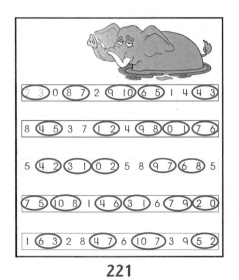

222

223

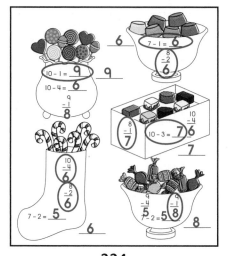

224

225

226

227

6 − 3 = 3	11 − 4 = 7	15 − 6 = 9	11 − 6 = 5			
12 − 3 = 9	10 − 6 = 4	12 − 4 = 8	10 − 5 = 5	13 − 5 = 8	8 − 7 = 1	12 − 3 = 9
14 − 8 = 6	17 − 9 = 8	11 − 8 = 3	15 − 7 = 8	14 − 9 = 5	10 − 3 = 7	13 − 4 = 9
9 − 6 = 3	12 − 9 = 3	14 − 6 = 8	8 − 5 = 3	12 − 7 = 5	18 − 9 = 9	14 − 6 = 8
8 − 5 = 3	12 − 7 = 5	18 − 9 = 9	14 − 6 = 8	13 − 8 = 5	13 − 6 = 7	17 − 8 = 9

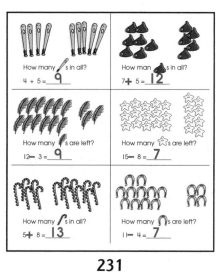

228

5 + 6 = 11   11 − 4 = 7
12 − 7 = 5   7 + 6 = 13
5 + 5 = 10   8 + 6 = 14

229

9 − 5 = 4   8 + 7 = 15   11 − 4 = 8   10 − 4 = 6
7 + 9 = 16   14 − 6 = 8   7 − 7 = 13

6 + 7 = 13   13 − 9 = 4
15 − 9 = 6   9 + 2 = 12
10 − 3 = 6   8 + 8 = 16

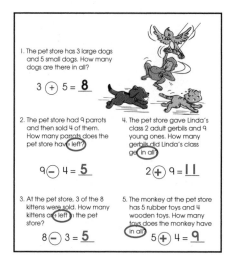

230

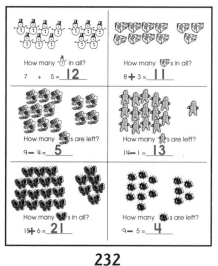

231

232

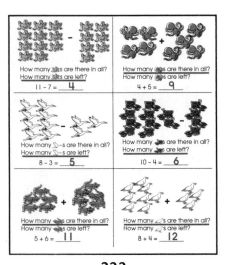

233

How many ...s are there in all?
How many ...s are left?
11 − 7 = **4**

How many ...s are there in all?
How many ...s are left?
4 + 5 = **9**

8 − 3 = **5**

10 − 4 = **6**

5 + 6 = **11**

8 + 4 = **12**

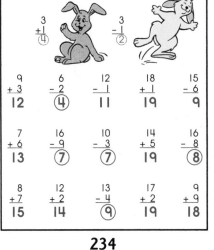

234

3 + 1 = (4)   3 − 1 = (2)

9 + 3 = 12   6 − 2 = (4)   12 − 1 = 11   18 + 1 = 19   15 − 6 = 9
7 + 6 = 13   16 − 9 = (7)   10 − 3 = (7)   14 + 5 = 19   16 − 8 = (8)
8 + 7 = 15   12 + 2 = 14   13 − 4 = (9)   17 + 2 = 19   9 + 9 = 18

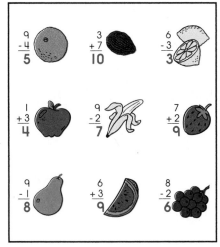

235

9 − 4 = 5   3 + 7 = 10   6 − 3 = 3
1 + 3 = 4   9 − 2 = 7   7 + 2 = 9
9 − 1 = 8   6 + 3 = 9   8 − 2 = 6

236

10 − 6 = 4   7 + 3 = 10   4 − 2 = 2   6 − 2 = 4   4 + 1 = 5
6 + 4 = 10   5 + 4 = 9   7 − 1 = 6   6 − 3 = 3
4 + 3 = 7   1 + 9 = 10   2 − 1 = 1   8 − 6 = 2   2 + 1 = 3   10 − 3 = 7   9 − 4 = 5
3 + 5 = 8   2 + 8 = 10   6 − 3 = 3   5 + 5 = 10   5 − 3 = 2   8 + 2 = 10   5 − 4 = 1
10 − 8 = 2   5 − 1 = 4   5 + 2 = 7   9 + 2 = 11   2 + 6 = 8   3 + 7 = 10   8 + 1 = 9

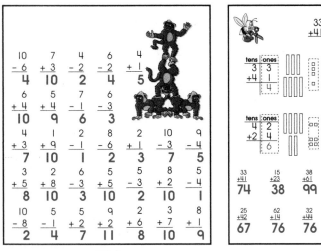

238

33 + 41   42 + 24

33 + 41 = 74   15 + 23 = 38   38 + 61 = 99   11 + 26 = 37   37 + 42 = 79   72 + 11 = 83
25 + 42 = 67   62 + 14 = 76   32 + 44 = 76   25 + 13 = 38   82 + 6 = 88   91 + 5 = 96

239

Example:
2 tens and 6 ones + 1 ten and 3 ones = 3 tens and 9 ones = 39

1 ten and 4 ones + 3 tens and 3 ones = **4** tens and **7** ones = **47**
2 tens and 5 ones + 2 tens and 3 ones = **4** tens and **8** ones = **48**
1 ten and 6 ones + 5 tens and 1 one = **6** tens and **7** ones = **67**
1 ten and 3 ones + 1 ten and 1 one = **2** tens and **4** ones = **24**
2 tens and 5 ones + 2 tens and 0 ones = **4** tens and **5** ones = **45**
1 ten and 5 ones + 2 tens and 4 ones = **3** tens and **9** ones = **39**
7 tens and 6 ones + 2 tens and 2 ones = **9** tens and **8** ones = **98**

240

tens	ones
2	4
+1	0
3	**4**

tens	ones
5	3
+3	2
8	**5**

tens	ones
7	1
+2	8
9	**9**

tens	ones
4	4
+3	2
7	**6**

tens	ones
5	1
+3	7
8	**8**

tens	ones
2	6
+5	2
7	**8**

tens	ones
2	6
+4	2
6	**8**

tens	ones
3	7
+5	1
8	**8**

tens	ones
1	9
+3	0
4	**9**

241

HOME 22 / VISITOR 17 — Total **39**
HOME 28 / VISITOR 30 — Total **58**
HOME 55 / VISITOR 21 — Total **76**
HOME 14 / VISITOR 33 — Total **47**
HOME 24 / VISITOR 13 — Total **37**
HOME 46 / VISITOR 32 — Total **78**
HOME 83 / VISITOR 06 — Total **89**
HOME 30 / VISITOR 20 — Total **50**
HOME 17 / VISITOR 42 — Total **59**
HOME 24 / VISITOR 45 — Total **69**

242

48	36	58	96	69	75	89	29
O	H	G	B	T	E	N	A

42 + 16 = 58   34 + 41 = 75   60 + 9 = 69   →   G E T
17 + 31 = 48   55 + 34 = 89   →   O N
26 + 43 = 69   14 + 22 = 36   52 + 23 = 75   →   T H E
83 + 13 = 96   24 + 24 = 48   5 + 24 = 29   52 + 17 = 69   →   B O A T!

B L A C K
B E A R E   J A M

243

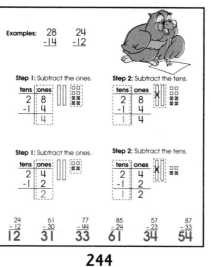

244

245

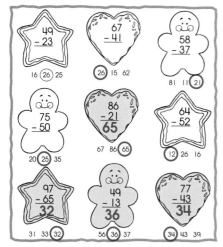

246

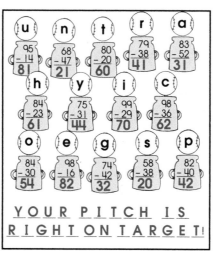

YOUR PITCH IS
RIGHT ON TARGET!

247

248

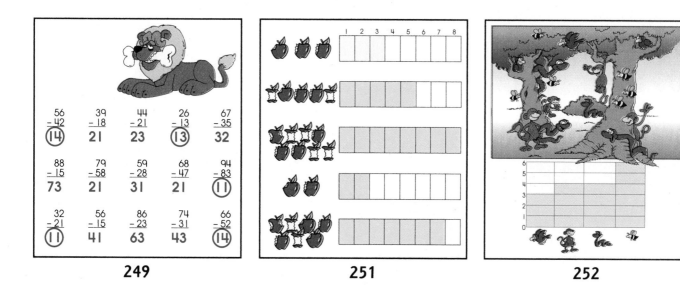

249

251

252

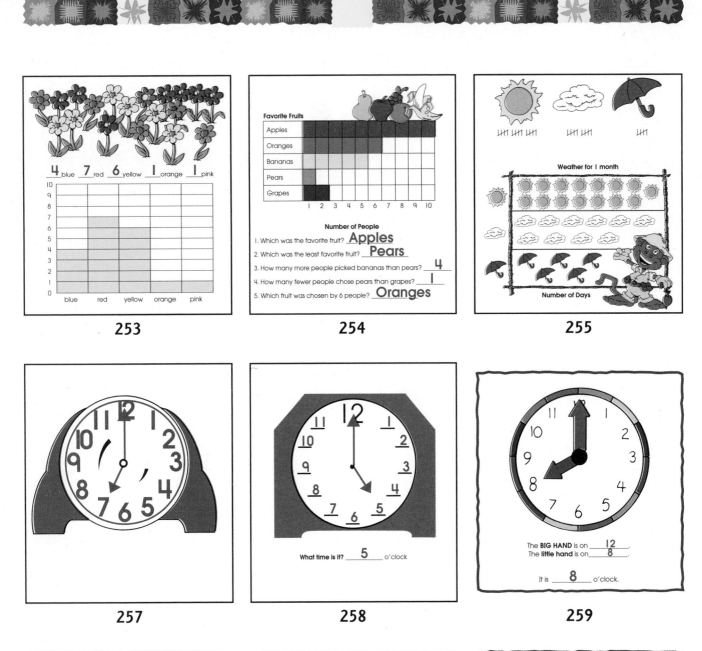

253

Flowers:
4 blue 7 red 6 yellow 1 orange 1 pink

254

Favorite Fruits

	1	2	3	4	5	6	7	8	9	10
Apples										
Oranges										
Bananas										
Pears										
Grapes										

Number of People

1. Which was the favorite fruit? **Apples**
2. Which was the least favorite fruit? **Pears**
3. How many more people picked bananas than pears? **4**
4. How many fewer people chose pears than grapes? **1**
5. Which fruit was chosen by 6 people? **Oranges**

255

Weather for 1 month

Number of Days

257

258

What time is it? **5** o'clock

259

The **BIG HAND** is on **12**
The **little hand** is on **8**

It is **8** o'clock.

260

4 o'clock   11 o'clock

5 o'clock

261

3 o'clock   **8** o'clock
4 o'clock   **12** o'clock
10 o'clock   **5** o'clock

262

8 o'clock   4 o'clock   2 o'clock
6 o'clock   11 o'clock   3 o'clock
1 o'clock   5 o'clock   7 o'clock

Answer Key

263

7 o'clock 12 o'clock 3 o'clock
6 o'clock 11 o'clock 1 o'clock
8 o'clock 4 o'clock 2 o'clock
9 o'clock 5 o'clock

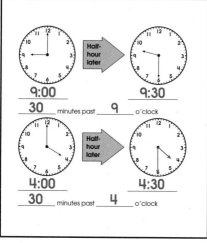

264

9:00 → Half-hour later → 9:30
30 minutes past 9 o'clock

4:00 → Half-hour later → 4:30
30 minutes past 4 o'clock

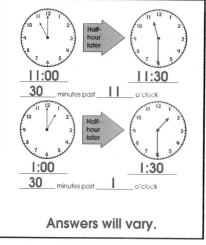

265

11:00 → Half-hour later → 11:30
30 minutes past 11 o'clock

1:00 → Half-hour later → 1:30
30 minutes past 1 o'clock

Answers will vary.

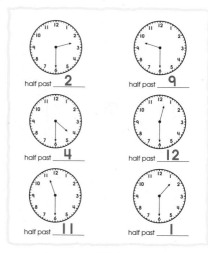

266

half past 2 half past 9
half past 4 half past 12
half past 11 half past 1

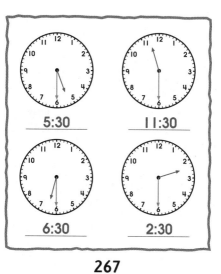

267

5:30 11:30
6:30 2:30

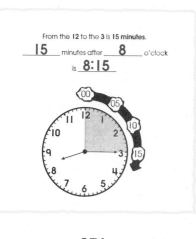

268

9:00 9:30   2:00 2:30
5:00 5:30   1:00 1:30
8:00 8:30   11:00 11:30

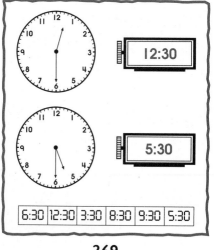

12:30

5:30

 6:30 12:30 3:30 8:30 9:30 5:30

269

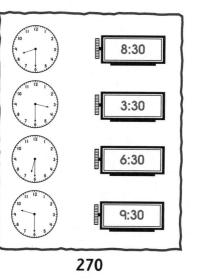

8:30

3:30

6:30

9:30

270

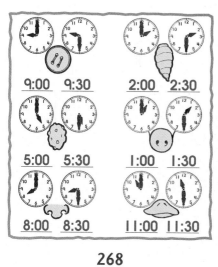

From the 12 to the 3 is 15 minutes.
15 minutes after 8 o'clock
is 8:15

271

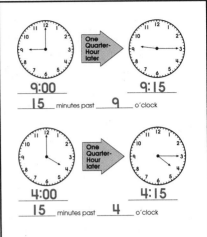

272

9:00
One Quarter-Hour later → 9:15
15 minutes past 9 o'clock

4:00
One Quarter-Hour later → 4:15
15 minutes past 4 o'clock

273

5:15
15 minutes after 5 o'clock

10:15
15 minutes after 10 o'clock

2:15
15 minutes after 2 o'clock

9:15
15 minutes after 9 o'clock

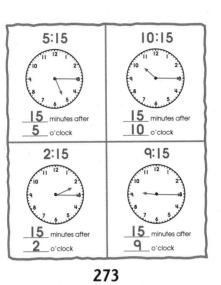

274

2:00   2:15
5:00   5:15
11:00 11:15
8:00   8:15

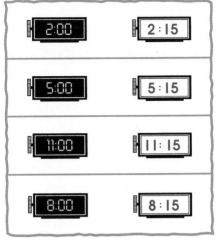

275

5:15 / 7:15
8:15 / 10:15
11:15 / 10:15
2:15 / 12:15
4:15 / 9:15
6:15 / 7:15
15 minutes after 6 o'clock

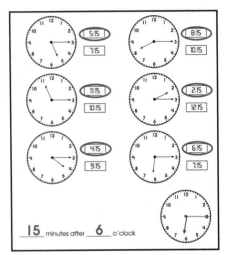

276

15 minutes after 12
30 minutes after 12
45 minutes after 12

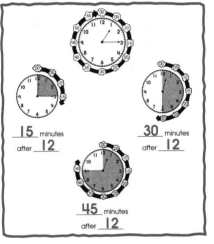

277

5:15 / 7:15
11:30 / 9:30
10:45 / 12:45
9:45 / 3:45
7:30 / 6:45
10:00 / 2:00
6:15 / 6:45
10:30 / 10:45
4:45 / 4:15
This pie bakes until a quarter past 4.

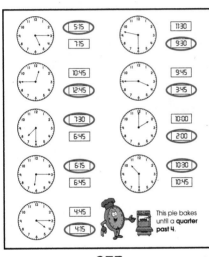

279

¢

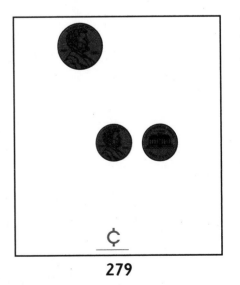

280

3 pennies = 3 ¢
5 pennies = 5 ¢
1 penny = 1 ¢
4 pennies = 4 ¢
2 pennies = 2 ¢

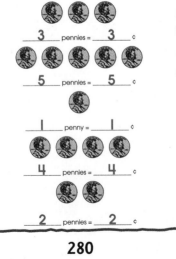

281

= 5 ¢   = 6 ¢
= 4 ¢   = 8 ¢

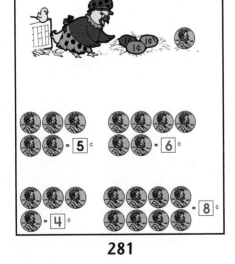

Answer Key

282

283

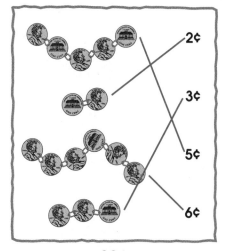

284

285

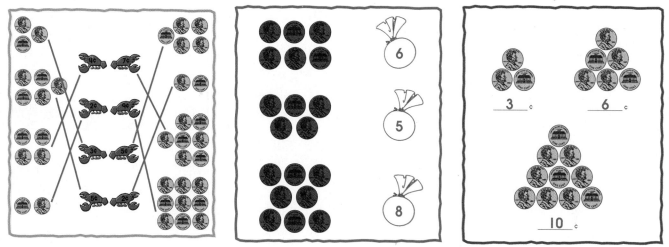

286

287

288

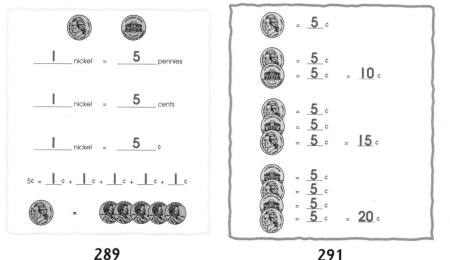

289

291

Answer Key

349

292

Count 5, 10, 15 — 15¢   Count 5, 10 — 10¢

Count 5, 10, 15 — 25¢   Count 5, 10, 15, 20 — 35¢
20, 25   25, 30, 35

Count 5, 10 — 20¢   Count 5, 10, 15 — 30¢
15, 20   20, 25, 30

293

20¢   25¢   10¢

30¢   15¢   5¢

35¢   45¢   40¢

294

25¢
30¢
20¢
35¢

295

20¢   10¢
30¢   35¢
15¢   45¢
40¢   25¢

296

25¢   35¢   40¢

297

17¢   14¢
21¢   9¢
13¢   27¢
18¢   16¢
31¢   19¢

298

5¢ + 1¢ = 6¢   5¢ + 3¢ = 8¢

5¢ + 4¢ = 9¢

5¢ + 6¢ = 11¢   5¢ + 2¢ = 7¢

299

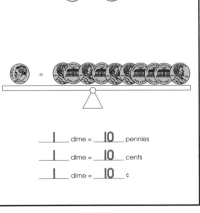

1 dime = 10 pennies
1 dime = 10 cents
1 dime = 10 ¢

300

30¢ or 10¢

40¢ or 30¢

50¢ or 90¢

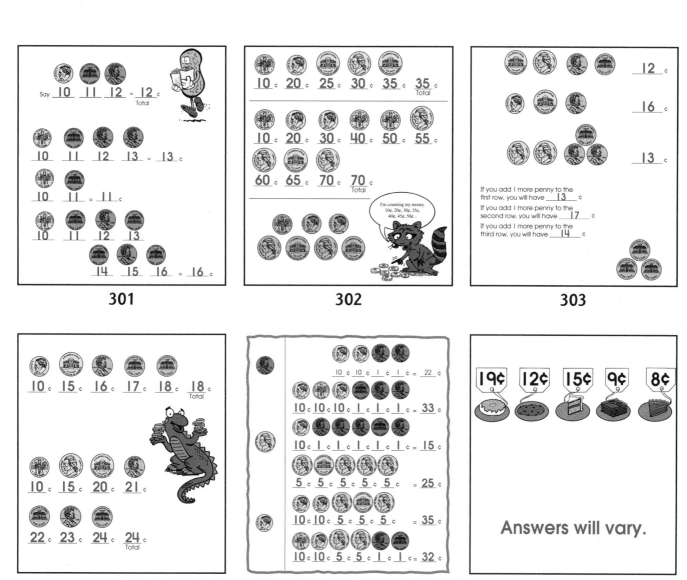

301 302 303

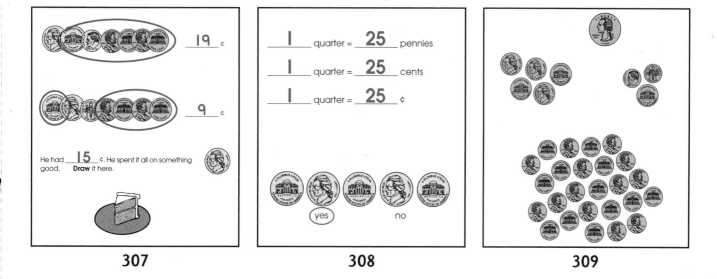

304 305 306

307 308 309

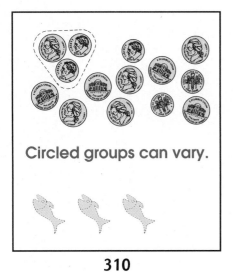

Circled groups can vary.

310

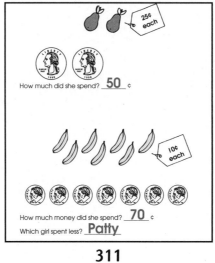

25¢ each

How much did she spend? **50** ¢

10¢ each

How much money did she spend? **70** ¢

Which girl spent less? **Patty**

311

25 ¢ 35 ¢ 45 ¢   **45** ¢
                      Total

25 ¢ 50 ¢ 55 ¢   **55** ¢
                      Total

Answer can vary.

312

25 ¢ 35 ¢ 40 ¢ 41 ¢ 42 ¢ **42** ¢
                              Total

25 ¢ 35 ¢ 45 ¢ 50 ¢ 55 ¢ **56** ¢

57 ¢ 58 ¢ **58** ¢
            Total

I'm counting my money.
25¢, 35¢, 45¢, 55¢, 60¢, 65¢, 66¢, 67¢.

1 quarter, 3 dimes, 2 nickels, and 2 pennies.

313

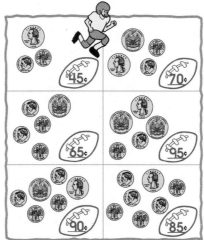

45¢   **70**¢

65¢   **95**¢

90¢   **85**¢

314